Dave Coffaro's *Leading from No* comprehension of change leadership imperatives and competencies required to an uncontested place few authors and / or consultants achieve! He clearly articulates decades of change management and agility navigation expertise into a clear roadmap for elevating strategy relevance and sustainability. David urges leaders to ascend every colleague's development and engagement to ultimately harness agility as a competitive differentiator in leading change. YES! Organizations who cultivate agility as a perpetual motion skill and place it within arm's reach for every human being will win!

Every leader who manifests this masterpiece theater of courageous leadership advice will transcend change management challenges with greater ease and value outcomes. This is a "great to exceptional" read for today's leader who wants to continuously position their organization to win amidst the ever-accelerating speed of now!"

Jayne C. Hladio, EVP, President Associated Bank Private Wealth

"In *Leading from Now*, Dave Coffaro lays out a provocative argument that challenges the reader to stop thinking about change management as an event and start leading change in a sustained, proactive manner. *Leading from Now* is a must read, serving as a practical guide for business owners and leaders looking to secure a competitive edge in a continuously evolving marketplace".

Maria Zlidar Richards, Director,
Mazda North American Operations

"*Leading from Now* is a great resource for anyone looking to make sure they don't allow their business model to slip into irrelevancy. Dave provides powerful insights and provocative questions to help ensure your business model doesn't become stale whether you own your own business, are leading a line of business, or are a leader in general."

Ben Alvarado, Executive Vice President, Director
of Core Banking, California Bank & Trust

Leading from Now isn't just a leadership guide; it's a captivating journey through the intricacies of change. Dave Coffaro's storytelling brings leadership principles to life in a way that's practical and relatable. The strategies shared are not just theoretical; they provide actionable steps for leaders facing the challenges of today's dynamic business landscape. Coffaro seamlessly blends history with contemporary relevance, offering a roadmap that's both authentic and inspiring. This book isn't a set of robotic instructions; it's a wisdom-infused guide, urging leaders to navigate change with confidence and resilience. Highly recommended for leaders seeking impact in an ever-evolving world."

Elzabeth Andrade, Executive Director, 211OC

As a new entrepreneur and co-founder of Adelphi Trust Company, I strongly recommend Dave Coffaro's newest book, *Leading from Now: A Leader's Guide to Navigating Change.* The book continues with Dave's helpful thoughts regarding when and how to redefine your business model to stay relevant and insights on developing your teams through business transformations. Change happens so fast in businesses today and there isn't a one and done process to work through but a continuing evolution for any company, even a regulated financial company. Dave provides engaging and entertaining examples that you can relate to your business. I commend Dave's book for any entrepreneur that wants to be prepared for the ever-changing business world we live in.

Gentry Barnett Byrnes, JD, Chief Fiduciary Officer
& Co-Founder, Adelphi Trust Company

Dave Coffaro's *Leading From Now* offers valuable insights into successfully navigating today's dynamic business environment. Grounded in practicality and real-life stories, the book resonates with authenticity, offering clear direction on crucial decisions and steps necessary for leaders to adapt and lead necessary change. I highly recommend it for anyone currently in or aspiring to a greater leadership role.

Peter Bielan, Founder, The Bielan Group

"Dave Coffaro's latest book, *Leading From Now: A Leader's Guide to Navigating Change* is an exemplary 'how-to' manual for all leaders in today's world. We are all navigating the ever increasing need to adapt quickly to a changing and highly competitive environment with best-in-class solutions and service. Leading and developing an agile business and workforce is critical for relevancy. This book not only explains the why, but also gives the how. Thank you, Dave!"

Diane Young, Chief Operating Officer,
Navy Federal Financial Group

With the unprecedented pace of change in modern business, steering an organization is not for the faint of heart! Leaders face challenges and opportunities in every aspect of their organizations. Whether it is global events and threats such as pandemics and climate change, urgent needs for racial and social justice, the evolving social media and digital landscape, or the integration of artificial intelligence (AI) tools, shifting conditions have had considerable impact on the activity of organizations and the people who work there. *Leading from Now: A Leader's Guide to Navigating Change* is an accessible and thought-provoking book that asks leaders to reflect, analyze, and gracefully lean into everything the future brings, especially change. As a business owner, I found Dave Coffaro's book inspiring—it created a sense of order and provided a calm approach for a time that can often feel chaotic. I have built my firm to ensure every customer has a consistently exemplary experience and this well-developed playbook makes that process navigable. Finally, Dave's experience-based examples make *A Leader's Guide to Navigating Change* relatable and a joy to read. Bravo!"

Shelli Herman, President and Founder,
Shelli Herman and Associates, Inc.

"Leadership requires intentionality, energy, and effort. Spent wisely, these will translate into an inspired and engaged organization. When allocated inappropriately the organization will falter. In an era of constant change and evolution, knowing when, where and how to take actions and make decisions has become more challenging than ever. In *Leading from Now,* Dave Coffaro pinpoints not only the mindset and mental clarity needed to lead in evolving times, but he also provides clear and relevant decisioning frameworks that foster sustained growth and success. Don't just buy the book and read it; use it as your personal blueprint for forward thinking leadership."

J. Phil Buchanan, Executive Chairman,
Cannon Financial Institute, Inc.

Leading from Now: A Leader's Guide to Navigating Change

David Coffaro

Leading from Now
A Leader's Guide to Navigating Change

© 2024 David Coffaro
All Rights Reserved
Published by SACG

ISBN: 978-1-734409925

Table of Contents

Foreword

Leading from Now: A Leader's Guide to Navigating Change emphasizes the importance for leaders to recognize the present moment is the only time from which to operate. Obvious? Yes and no. Consider management financial reports. Most organizations, boards of directors, and financial analysts evaluate year-to-date financial results, year-over-year comparisons, and historic trend-lines. This information is important, but its' value decreases daily. By the time a finance manager completes a business's year-end reports in January of the following year, the performance of activities which created the results might have taken place twelve months prior. How much do customers, their views, preferences, priorities change over twelve months? How much do employees change in a year? How different is technology supporting a business each year?

Now is the operative. The dictionary tells us *now* means at the present moment. And the present moment is always new. Following "if-then" logic, as *Leading from Now* means leading in the present moment, and the present moment is always new, organizations must be grounded in what *is* (current realty) and *what is unfolding* in their business (evolving customers, changing talent management conditions, new technology requirements). Recognizing the future starts now, and by definition is different than the past, competency Navigating Change is fundamental to every leader's role.

Effective navigation requires a clear destination (applied to business, a success destination, or "vision") and initial route (strategy). Effective navigators understand conditions in their journey are in perpetual motion, requiring continuous refinement of their route. This understanding - conditions are always in motion – recognizes the status quo is the *current* state of affairs in *this* moment, not an immutable set of circumstances. Absent understanding that business operating conditions are in perpetual motion, leaders can be lulled into perceiving change management as an event instead of an ongoing process, a special project in contrast to a core job function. Change Leadership recognizes change navigation as business as usual. Change Leaders develop organizational agility which enables the navigator to observe continually evolving conditions, adapt their route in alignment with their destination, and continue adjustment throughout their journey.

The principles in *Leading from Now: A Leader's Guide to Navigating Change* are like those embodied in successful navigation. This guide is inspired by research, observation, and experience navigating change. I believe a first step in elevating change leadership competency is developing a mindset which recognizes perpetual motion as normal. From this foundation, the question is not "what do we do when business conditions change?", instead, it is "how do we best position our organization now in light of the continually evolving operating environment?" Much more than semantics, each question comes from a substantively different cognitive approach to change.

My work focuses on guiding people and organizations in navigating change. That means I too am a student of how best to practice agility in a perpetually changing world. I am blessed to be surrounded by wonderful people who inspire me, teach me, and challenge me to be my best self, personally and professionally, with family at the top of this list. Carrie, Michael, Nicole, thank you for sharing ideas, reading outlines and excerpts, and your candid feedback. Carrie, thank you for encouraging me to write this book. Nicole, thank you for being the subject of so many entertaining stories. Michael, thank you for suggesting the addition of *Leading from Now* to my original *A Leader's Guide to Navigating Change*.

To my colleagues and clients – I am blessed by the abundance of lessons and opportunities you share. Lee Pound, I admire your attention to detail and constructive coaching. Rob Kirby, each time you create a book cover, I think it's your best yet; I'm excited to see the next one. I share my deep gratitude to the business leaders who generously invested time to review *Leading from Now* – Ben Alvarado, Executive Vice President, Director of Core Banking, California Bank & Trust; Elizabeth Andrade, Executive Director, 211OC; Gentry Barnett Byrnes, Co-Founder & Chief Fiduciary, Officer, Adelphi Trust; Peter Bielan, Founder, The Bielan Group; J. Phil Buchanan, Executive Chairman, Cannon Financial Institute, Inc.; Shelli Herman, President and Founder, Shelli Herman and Associates, Inc.; Jayne C. Hladio, EVP, President, Associated Bank Private Wealth; Maria Zlidar Richards, Director, Mazda North American Operations; and Diane Young, Chief Operating Officer, Navy Federal Financial Group.

Introduction

The year 1960 was more than the beginning of a new decade. In the United States, it opened an era of youthful energy, growing abundance, and social and environmental awareness. First born Baby Boomers turned fourteen that year. Their parents spent discretionary income on entertainment for their kids.

Four years earlier, Elvis Presley became the first global rock star (four years later, The Beatles would make their first appearance on the Ed Sullivan show). Elvis held two places on Billboard's 1960 Hot 100 songs ("It's Now or Never" and *Stuck on You*" and top selling album of the year with *G.I. Blues*. Chubby Checkers hit the #1 spot on Billboard's Hot 100 in September with *The Twist*, and Surf Music entered the mainstream with the Ventures *Walk, Don't Run*. The year saw outstanding record sales. In the same year, Russ Solomon started Tower Records in Sacramento, California.

Solomon's father ran Tower Drugs on Broadway in Sacramento, filling prescriptions, selling cosmetics, toys, liquor, and magazines. The drug store included a soda fountain popular with a teenage audience, in part due to a jukebox that played popular 78 RPM records.

Solomon Senior theorized his store could sell used jukebox records in the drug store. He negotiated the purchase of used records from his jukebox vendor at three cents apiece, then resold them for a dime. The experiment succeeded, he sold out all records in inventory immediately. Solomon decided that since used records sold so quickly, Tower Drugs could sell new records at a similar pace. He negotiated a deal with record wholesalers to buy new records at a heavily discounted price and jumped into the growing retail music business.

Russ Solomon, a teenager at the time, volunteered to lead Tower Records. From 1960 through the mid 1990s Tower was the preeminent music retailer, known as the go-to place for the best selection and largest inventory of records across all musical genres.

Iconic Tower Records stores emerged on Sunset Boulevard in Hollywood, Greenwich Village in New York, and Nashville, Tennessee. At peak, the company operated 220 retail stores, making Tower Records the largest music retailer in the United States. Eventually Tower expanded outside the United States with stores in Japan, Taiwan, the U.K. and beyond.

Tower Records became the place to get the latest album releases, sometimes at a midnight event attended by a musician promoting their new work. Artists often showed up at Tower Records stores for an informal performance or album signing session. The atmosphere was more like a party than an old school retail establishment.

The pace of change in the music industry accelerated between the 1980s and the early 2000s. Preferences of music buyers evolved. Technology advanced. New listening media emerged. Long play record albums gave way to digital compact discs, digital music file sharing (Napster), digital downloads (iTunes), and eventually Spotify, Sound Cloud, YouTube, and Tik Tok. Customers preferred to buy a single song rather than spend money on an album that included selections they might not like.

The nature and intensity of competition shifted from primarily other record stores to large format retailers like Best Buy, Wal-Mart, Target, and K-mart, who often deployed a loss-leader strategy, pricing CD's near or below their cost to increase store traffic.

As their operating environment evolved, Tower Records' financial performance deteriorated. Revenue for 1999 exceeded $1 billion. From that point, sales declined. At the same time, the company's balance sheet showed $110 million in high interest debt.

Even with a clear view of evolving operating conditions, Russ Solomon believed people would always want to buy records and grow their physical music library. Company leaders failed to embrace new technologies and music delivery formats, convinced that customers would continue to buy physical CDs. But consumers just wanted the music; they didn't seem to care about owning a record or CD.

In 2006 Tower Records filed for bankruptcy. Company leaders failed to navigate a changed business environment. Change momentum accelerated for customers, competition, and technology. Management observed movement yet failed to infer what it meant to the company and its outdated go-to-market business model.

A *Forbes*[1] article November 15th of that year said, "With the music buying experience evolving by the moment, old-fashioned record stores with leases, staff and high inventory costs (tying up millions in capital), needed a drastic overhaul. That left Tower with the have-it-all-in-stock business model, the go-to source for hard-nosed music enthusiasts. But taking that model seriously demanded aggressive increases in inventories and tight working relations with distributors, rather than dropping every CD that didn't sell once in six months.

---

[1] https://www.forbes.com/2006/11/15/tower-music-bankruptcy-oped-cx_jfl_1115tower.html?sh=405b58e97975

"Perhaps the dynamic of a corporate hierarchy under stress, self-preservation over problem solving, connections outweighing merit, fresh thinking discouraged. made a serious recovery effort impossible. That would have demanded closing the money-losing smaller stores, investing heavily in the two dozen or so profitable outlets in big markets and covering key [music] genres in overwhelming depth…In other words, *create* a market, don't just put stuff on the shelves and open the doors."

The Forbes article concluded, "Tower's management, mistaking 'vision' for acumen, slept through the revolution, making gestures toward the new music retailing landscape but doing too little too late."

Tower Records' story is not unique. The company's rise and fall personifies the criticality of effective change navigation and provides an abundance of actionable lessons. Right now, at this moment, whatever the business:

- **Customers change**. Who they are, what they value, and what they expect now is different than five years ago and different than it will be over the next five years.
- **Competition changes.** Firms you compete with, how you compete (price, offering, engagement approach, technology), intensity of competition, alternatives, and substitute offerings available are in flux.
- **How businesses engage with customers changes**. Interfaces with customers (human interaction, physical sales/service locations, self-service, technology platforms) digital connectivity, customer acquisition marketing (digital, social, other) and ongoing engagement are all in motion.
- **Employees change**. Who they are, what they value, what they expect from your firm, and your firm's value

proposition to employees are different now than five years ago and will be five years hence.

- **Technology supporting business changes**. Core platforms required to operate the business are different today than over the past five years. The technology horizon over the next few years is evolving. Business processes will need to be refined or redesigned to enhance operational efficiency.

- **Economics of a business change**. Staffing, supplies, transportation, premises, technology, insurance, and tax costs are dynamic. How will the next five years differ from the previous, and what impact will that have on pricing and profitability?

Each of these change domains affected the Tower Records story. From the time of the company's founding to 1999, its peak revenue year, the retail music business underwent dramatic shifts.

When Tower Records opened for business in 1960, predominant music media options were 33 1/3rd, 45, and 78 revolution per minute records and live AM radio. In the late 1960s, FM radio emerged as the place for album-oriented rock music, creating a venue for the introduction of new musical styles. Cassette and 8-track tapes became popular formats for portable music in the 1970s. Disco music became mainstream later in the decade, and British-influenced punk rock gained notoriety. A decade later, tape-based formats lost share to the compact disc, introduced in 1982.

The 1980s also represented changing customers. While Baby Boomers still bought disco and rap, Gen X customers became a market segment with different musical tastes and purchasing patterns than their elders. Hip Hop, New Wave, Synth-pop, and Alternative Rock grew in popularity. First wave rock and roll lost some of the luster it held when Tower Records began.

The 1990s began a period of accelerated change for the music business. The first Millennials entered their teen years. Technology and how consumers listened to music advanced at an accelerated pace. The first portable MP3 player launched in 1997. Amazon began selling music and videos in 1998. In early 2001, Apple launched iTunes. Two years later the iTunes Store opened, selling music for 99 cents per song, driving a significant paradigm shift in the way people consumed digital media and the economics of the music business.

Management's decisions to ignore, minimize or rationalize four decades of continually changing operating conditions and business operating model implications had a deleterious effect on the company's relevance, pertinence, and importance to its customers.

In a previous book, *Leading from Zero, Seven Essential Elements of Earning Relevance*, I wrote about the way in which organizations earn and sustain relevance with customers, employees, and partners:

"Many factors contribute to organizational longevity, perhaps none more than relevance with stakeholders: employees, customers, partners, and vendors. Earning and sustaining relevance - pertinence, meaningfulness, importance - is a leader's ongoing responsibility. Relevance decays when overlooked. Organizations that slip into irrelevance face the difficult task of re-earning standing with employees, customers, and other stakeholders, or riding a cycle of demise.

"Every organization starts its day from a base of *zero*. Zero customers. Zero employees. Zero revenue. Leaders must influence their organizations and *earn relevance* with customers, employees, and other stakeholders every day. Organizations have no entitlement to customers, employees, or revenue. Customers and employees have free will and only engage with an organization that demonstrates a relevant vision and clear value proposition and continually delivers on both. For leaders, a fundamental question is, "How will I earn relevance today?"

Leading from Now: A Leader's Guide to Navigating Change builds on the importance of earning and sustaining relevance as an *outcome* of effective *change leadership*, beginning with a set of foundational principles:

- Change Leadership refers to proactive, ongoing adaptation of an organization to its operating environment, which is in perpetual motion.
- Change Leadership *is* strategic management, an ongoing, dynamic process.
- Leaders must be attuned to conditions in the present moment to infer and inform actions taken today, aligned with future success.
- Business go-to-market operating models have a finite shelf-life, and require regular refreshment, refinement, or replacement.
- Leaders decide to intentionally initiate change or react to forces evolving the organization.
- The next phase of "normal" is a continually evolving story for each organization to write.
- Vision sets the course, informs actions defined by the operating model.
- Simplicity strengthens strategy.

A fundamental business reality underlays these principles - *operating conditions are in perpetual motion.* Dynamic, evolving, chaotic - whatever term you chose to describe the business operating environment, the essence is continuous change. While leaders are accustomed to reciting, "Nothing is certain but change," few organizations are proficient in navigating ongoing change.

Companies gather geobytes of customer data, employee engagement insights, and the latest industry-specific technology trend details, then fall short translating this information to evolve their go-to-market business models. But there is another approach.

Therefore, in contrast to the view that *change management* is an event, or series of events, *leading change* is an ongoing, dynamic process.

This book is written for organizations and their leaders (owners, team leaders, division leaders, executive directors, CEOs) adjusting to a rapidly changing environment, those in transition, companies revisiting their future state success definition, and groups underperforming expectations. I offer guidance to elevate your change leadership acumen, and consequently better positions you to develop and deploy adaptive business operating models that bring your organization's vision to life.

We will explore the shelf-life of business operating models, model management, overcoming challenges associated with leading change, how to develop agility as an organizational competency, and team member engagement as a fundamental element of navigating change in for profit business and in the nonprofit sector.

Introduction

Leading from Now: A Leader's Guide to Navigating Change includes a set of resources to help you assess your organization: the Operating Model Refresh Urgency Indicators, Change Guidance Framework, and Change Leadership Opportunity Assessment.

My purpose in writing this book is to provide actionable ideas to help leaders address one of the most prevalent challenges facing all types of organizations – navigating change. I hope *Leading from Now: A Leader's Guide to Navigating Change* becomes a valuable resource for you and your firm!

Chapter 1
What is the Shelf Life of Normal?

Thursday, October 31, 2013, is not a date that stands out in the minds of most Americans. Sure, it was Halloween. But beyond trick-or-treaters, their parents, and candy manufacturers, this specific date wasn't anything special— unless you were a frequent flyer.

From the time cell phones were commercially introduced in 1983, airlines required that these devices be turned off during a flight. The impetus for this regulation was the concern that cellular devices might interfere with an airplane's avionics and navigation systems. But 30 years later, the Federal Aviation Administration put out press release 13010, "Expanding Use of Passenger Portable Electronic Devices." The FAA determined airlines could safely allow passengers to use portable electronic devices such as cell phones during all phases of flight. The announcement explained that due to differences among fleets and operations, implementation would vary among airlines. All things considered, the agency anticipated that all carriers would safely implement the new rule for cellular use in airplane mode, gate-to-gate, by the end of the year.

As a frequent business traveler, I often begin my week in an airplane. November 4, 2013, was no exception. My first flight went from Santa Ana to Phoenix on Southwest Airlines. As the flight pushed back from the gate, the flight attendant announced that due to an exciting FAA rule change, passengers could now leave their cell phones on during the flight if we made sure we switched our device into airplane mode.

That Tuesday, I flew on a second airline from Phoenix to Minneapolis. I heard no announcement during boarding or in flight about the new cell phone rule, and not a word from the crew.

Wednesday, on my third airline trip of the week I flew from Minneapolis to Dallas. Many passengers knew about the new FAA rule, and during boarding the flight attendant fielded question after question about leaving cell phones on during the flight. Exasperated, he made an announcement over the PA system: "We just learned about an FAA rule change on cell phone use last week. The airline is evaluating the rule change and will let passengers know what it means as soon as possible, but for now turn your cell phones completely off during this flight."

Thursday, I flew back home from Dallas with the same airline I took the day before. This time, at the gate, the counter agent announced that the airline hadn't developed a plan to implement the new FAA rule.

With this regulation, "normal" was redefined on October 31, 2013 — at least relative to portable electronic device use in airplanes. Southwest Airlines' vision is to be the world's most loved, most efficient, and most profitable airline. One value that drives the company to fulfill its vision is simple: *Stay agile*. Agility is part of how Southwest succeeds as it continually redefines normal. The airline's quick adaptation to and communication of the new FAA rule demonstrated this.

The shelf life of *normal* is infinitesimally short. Whether we're discussing the business environment or personal activities in daily life, the definition of normal is in perpetual motion, though speed can vary. How could it be different? Life is motion. We live on a planet revolving at a speed of 1,000 miles an hour, traversing the sun at an estimated 70,000 miles an hour. Individual perspectives, beliefs, and priorities of the 8 billion people on the planet aggregate into collective views, always in flux. A decade ago, IBM Watson used to identify emotion patterns in groups by analyzing social media posts. One finding: collective emotions always change. Today's artificial intelligence tools reinforce this axiom to understand and anticipate consumer behavior. The nature of normal life is motion.

Consider the extraordinary impact of the COVID-19 pandemic on business. In 2021, according to Gallup's *State of the Global Workplace Report*, almost one out of three working people on the planet - just over 1 billion adults - lost their job or business because of the coronavirus situation. Normal in the business environment redefined itself in early 2020 as the impact of the pandemic unfolded. Businesses that survived or thrived did so under a new, rapidly evolving definition of normal. Demand, supply, supply chains, manufacturing, logistics, workforces, worker availability, transportation, and most aspects of the global economy experienced multiple redefinitions of normal.

In the post-COVID era, normal was redefined many times. Work from home. Return to work. Hybrid work. Quiet quit work. Redefine work. Digital First. High Touch. Outsource. Insource. Reshore. Still, there is talk about returning to normal, or the new normal, as though it is a destination. While an extraordinary episode (like a global pandemic) can stimulate a desire to reach the next stability plateau, normal is a continually unfolding context, constantly being redefined. What we perceive as normal is simply a point on a continuum of dynamic change to which we become accustomed. Ergo, normal must be continually redefined.

Redefining Normal while Leading from Now

Leading from Now includes recognizing the need for unceasingly redefining normal and building on this reality to guide the organization in earning and sustaining relevance - pertinence, meaningfulness, importance - with employees, customers, and all stakeholders. Leaders need to ask, "What comes next for this organization, and what will it take for our company to earn and sustain relevance with our stakeholders tomorrow?"

The next phase of normal is a constantly evolving story for each organization to write, beginning now. But, if normal is in flux, where can leaders and their organizations find stability? In the business world, the answer lies in the organization's vision and values, which guide people and priorities and inform strategy execution when the definition of normal is in perpetual motion.

Vision is the company's answer to the question: what does success look like for us? It's not esoteric or amorphous. It is simply how an organization defines success. Meaningful vision statements are:

- **Aspirational** – Future-focused picture of how your organization will contribute to the world.
- **Inspirational** – Team members feel motivated to play a role in bringing the vision to life.
- **Meaningful** – Each day, team members determine how to align their decisions and actions toward vision fulfilment.

Vision is a touchstone for stability in an environment in perpetual motion. While customers, employees, competitors, and technology change, the vision stays relatively stable. It provides context for people within an organization to adapt to their changing operating environment. These sample vision statements meet the aspirational, inspirational, and meaningful criteria:

- **Amazon**: To be Earth's most customer-centric company, Earth's best employer, and Earth's safest place to work.
- **Southwest Airlines:** To be the world's most loved, most efficient, and most profitable airline.
- **LEGO:** A global force of learning through play.
- **Zoom:** Communications empowering people to accomplish more.
- **Feeding America:** A hunger-free America.
- **Smithsonian:** Shaping the future by preserving our heritage, discovering new knowledge, and sharing our resources with the world.
- **TED**: Spread ideas.

The first question I ask in a consulting engagement is: How does your organization define success? Leaders often respond with sales goals, profitability metrics, or growth goals. These are all aspects of how a firm measures results, but not the definition of success, as the examples above illustrate.

Values are an organization's core principles and beliefs that guide its priorities, actions, decisions, and define culture. When values synchronize with the company's vision, they create a strong sense of belonging for team members. Clearly defined value pillars put into words what the company cares about and inform appropriate organizational behavior; they also shine a bright light on misaligned activities and choices. This means organizations just paying lip service to stated values will appear inauthentic. Examples of value pillars are integrity, teamwork, diversity and inclusion, customer centricity, and contribution to the greater good.

Demonstrated values provide a roadmap to guide the organization in navigating challenges and opportunities while remaining aligned with its vision. Because values create a sense of unity and purpose, they contribute to a feeling of stability in an environment in perpetual motion.

Leading from Now means everything the leader does is aligned with the company's vision and values to guide people and priorities. Absent a clear vision, organizations, processes, and leaders inevitably drift from their goals. Without demonstrating a consistent set of values, employees can feel uncertain and unclear about what the company stands for. With a clear vision and values, organizations can find comfort in uncertainty, grounding through change and stability in progress. In an environment where normal is continually redefined, stability and strategic resilience stem from alignment with the organization's vision and values.

In today's reality, the shortest measurement of time is known as the zeptosecond — one trillionth of a billionth of a second, or a decimal point followed by 20 zeroes and a 1. While not scientifically supported, I suggest the shelf life of normal is close to a zeptosecond, requiring leaders to make the redefinition of normal core to their practice.

Chapter 2
How to Know When It's Time to Change

In 1938, Clarence Leonidas (Leo) Fender opened Fender's Radio Service in Fullerton, California. Leo started out repairing radios, record players, public address systems and musical instrument amplifiers. As with many innovators, Leo saw an opportunity to improve on existing products in the marketplace, in particular, amplifiers.

In 1945, building on several years of repair work, amplifier design, and development of an electric Hawaiian lap steel guitar, Leo formed a partnership with Clayton Kauffman to manufacture musical instrument amplifiers and lap steel guitars. At the end of the partnership's first year in business, Leo wanted to focus his energy on electric instrument and amplifier manufacturing, so he separated from partner Kauffman and renamed his business the Fender Electric Instrument Company.

Over the next two decades, Leo Fender masterfully observed and satisfied a growing demand for affordable, playable electric guitars. Before Fender's market entrance, most electric guitars were hand-built and expensive, placing them out of reach for many musicians. Leo designed and mass produced innovative, cool looking, affordable guitars. In 1950, he introduced the Broadcaster (eventually renamed the Telecaster), which became the world's first commercially successful solid-body electric guitar. He followed this approach with the introduction of the

Precision Bass in 1951, Stratocaster in 1954, Jazzmaster in 1959, Jazz Bass in 1961 and Jaguar in 1962.

The 1960s was an era of significant change in the pop music industry. As with Tower Records, Fender benefited from affluent teenaged Baby Boomers, rock and roll, and broad access to popular music. Leo, an astute marketer, targeted young musicians and captured their attention with Fender guitars featured on record covers, in movies and on television shows, solidifying their cool factor. Fender also developed strong artist relationships, working closely with well-known musicians to develop signature guitars and amplifiers, which helped to keep the brand at the forefront of popular music. This close connection to his customer base enabled Fender to remain attuned and adaptive to evolving interests, preferences, and the competitive environment.

Leo sold Fender Musical Instruments Corporation in 1965 for health reasons (an interesting story in-and-of-itself; later, in good health, Leo re-entered the business and built two more instrument companies – Music Man and G&L Guitars). Over the years, Fender faced a continually changing operating environment. Demand for their products (musical instruments overall) has ebbed and flowed. The competitive environment presented challenges as lower cost and high-end alternatives flooded the market. Musical trends shifted many times and are in transition to this day.

Fender Musical Instrument Corporation today demonstrates agility and adaptability as their operating environment evolves. Fender expanded its product line to include acoustic guitars, basses, amplifiers, and pro audio equipment. It also embraced new technologies, such as digital modeling and online sales.

The company is *Leading from Now*. Andy Mooney has served as CEO since June 2015. In a recent interview, Mooney discussed the company's customer base, its diversity, and how Fender stays attuned to the evolving operating environment. "Fender caters to so many genres. The reason that Leo Fender's designs have stood the test of time is because he listened to feedback from working musicians. He designed the platforms to cater to their needs on the road. So, they have very versatile instruments that you can play in any genre.

"When I joined the company, I was hungry for data. Everybody in the company had an opinion about who was buying our products, but nobody had any data. So [Fender Chief Marketing Officer] Evan Jones and I conducted what I believe is the most comprehensive piece of research the industry ever did. And the five key insights that emerged shaped almost everything we've done over the last five years. One is that 45% of the guitars that we sell every year went to a first-time player, much higher than we thought. Fifty percent of those first-time players were women. A huge aha. Then, 90% of first-time players abandon the instrument in the first year, if not the first 90 days, but the 10% who don't abandon the instrument have a lifetime value of roughly $10,000." This insight positioned Fender to explore how to convert novice guitar players into lifelong musicians. Mooney added, "If we could reduce the abandonment rate by just 10%, we could double the hardware sales over time."

Deep understanding of its customers guided Fender to align products and offers accordingly, offering entry level guitars and basses at a price point of $200 - $600 and high-end Custom Shop offerings at $2,500+ targeted to more experienced and affluent players.

In earlier days, Fender relied on its retail dealers and allocated all its $16 million marketing budget to outlets like Guitar Center and other music retailers. Mooney said, "From a consumer's perspective, our new product introductions were like trees falling in the forest. The only people who knew about them were the in-store sales associates. Demonstrating the importance of *Leading from Now*, Mooney brought on a chief digital products officer and introduced Fender Play, a video-oriented mobile teaching app for guitar, bass, and ukulele.

In early 2020, as Covid unfolded, the $10 a month app had 110,000 subscribers. Understanding his customers and the opportunity at hand, Mooney offered Fender Play free for 30 days. One week later, the number of subscribers doubled. By midyear 2020, close to a million users had registered for Fender Play, and began receiving Fender product and promotional emails and social media offers. Fender targets its current $100 million advertising budget to its consumer, primarily through social media.

Cues and Clues

Albert Einstein said, "The measure of intelligence is the ability to change." What he didn't elaborate on is knowing when it's time to change. Fender's Andy Mooney knew his team needed to refine the company's go-to-market model. Fender's customers were changing (growing diversity across age groups, gender, cultures, musical tastes, economic characteristics, and skill levels). What they needed was changing (e.g. online, easy to access, on-demand music lessons to increase player engagement), and how to engage with existing and prospective customers (digital and social media vs. promotion through retail music stores) were all in motion. Mooney and Fender's leadership team made moves to advance the company in alignment with current reality, understanding they operate in a dynamic environment (translation: in perpetual motion, therefore requiring ongoing refinement).

Change stimuli emerge in two manners – Systemic and Non-systemic cues. Systemic change cues impact all organizations – inflation, national or global economic expansion or contraction, tax code changes, pandemics, geopolitical issues, and the like. Non-systemic change cues are unique to a specific organization or industry. For instance: the patent on a company's flagship product expires next year allowing competitors to replicate that specific offering, or a new federal regulatory capital requirement impacts all banks.

A *Leading from Now* practice is to identify relevant cues, then delve into underlying details to determine a level of urgency to address each condition:

Changing Demand

- What changes do you anticipate in your customer base over the next two to three years (demographics, geographic, economics)?
- What changes do you anticipate in customer expectations of your offering over the next two to three years (product, technology, ease of use, features, quality, pricing)?
- What have you tracked/observed with changes in customer satisfaction/engagement over the past two to three years?
- How has your customer attrition rate changed over the past two to three years?
- How has your flow of new customers changed over the past two to three years?

- What trends have you observed in the number of repeat customers over the past two to three years?
- What are the themes and volume associated with customer complaints over the past two to three years (including unfavorable online and social media traffic)?

Changing Supply

- What changes do you anticipate in employee expectations for your business over the next two to three years (evolution of the company's value proposition to employees, career and professional development, benefits, compensation)?
- How do you anticipate the talent pool (early, mid-career, seasoned talent) and competition for talent changing over the next two to three years?
- What have you tracked/observed with trend changes in employee engagement over the past two to three years?
- What was your level of employee attrition (regrettable, encouraging) over the past two to three years? How does this level align with your expectations?
- What themes and volume are associated with employee complaints over the past two to three years?
- What changes do you anticipate in suppliers over the next two to three years (supply chain changes, new suppliers, product offering, industry consolidation, technology, costs, pricing)?
- What types of non-systemic (e.g., unrelated to COVID-19) supplier service/delivery issues have you experienced over the past two to three years? What is the cause?

Changing Customer Engagement Approaches

- What changes do you anticipate in how your company interfaces with customers (human interaction, physical sales/service locations, self-service, digital platforms)?
- What changes do you anticipate in the availability of on-demand customer engagement offerings (accessing your products or services where, when, and how the customer prefers)?
- What changes do you anticipate in the competitive landscape (new entrants, consolidation, new products, new technology, pricing changes) over the next two to three years, and how will these impact your business?
- What changes do you anticipate in how aggressively competitors pursue your customers over the next two to three years?
- What changes do you anticipate in your operating economics over the next two to three years?

Changing Technology

- What changes in technology do you anticipate will support your business operations (including sourcing, transportation, manufacturing, human resources, finance and accounting, and marketing) over the next two to three years?
- What changes do you anticipate in the technology required to serve your customers?
- What changes do you anticipate in technology to engage with your suppliers and vendors?

Competition

- What changes do you anticipate in the competitive landscape (new entrants, consolidation, new products, new technology, pricing changes) over the next three years and how will these impact your business?
- What changes do you anticipate in how aggressively competitors pursue your clients over the next three years?
- What changes do you anticipate in your operating economics over the next three years?

This partial list of change cues suggests how leaders can evaluate the need and address evolving conditions with urgency. In the next chapter, we discuss how these cues inform refresh, refinement, or reengineering of your business operating model. Knowing when to initiate change is essential in navigating change leadership.

Regardless of the change stimulus, in the business world leaders are called upon to anticipate and address their continually evolving environment for the benefit of their stakeholders. This means embracing the reality that business operating conditions are in perpetual motion. Those who do not heed the call to lead change as an ongoing process may jeopardize their organization's future.

Chapter 3
Has Your Business Model Exceeded its Shelf Life?

"Within five years, if you're in the same business you are in now, you're going to be out of business." — Peter Drucker

Imagine New Year's Eve, three years from now. While you're getting ready to ring in the new year with family and friends, you take a few minutes and reflect on the year now ending. As you think back over the past 12 months, a question comes to mind: *What did I do as a leader that had the greatest impact on my business this year?* Leading operating reviews? Developing new products? Analyzing financial performance? Coaching direct reports? Recruiting new talent? Each of these activities matter, but their impact will be suboptimal if your business model is stale.

Every business operating model has a finite shelf-life, which at some point loses effectiveness as, over time, the operating environment changes. It's easy to see with examples like Blockbuster Video. Customer expectations for video content shifted from physical, retail store access to on-demand and eventually streaming. Alternative content delivery options, formats, and providers (Netflix, Amazon Prime Video, Hulu, Disney+ to name a few) became available. Then a global pandemic created an extraordinary accelerant in the evolution of entertainment content access. Changes in demand, supply, technology. and customer delivery alternatives all advanced the obsolescence of the retail video store business operating model.

Operating Conditions in Perpetual Motion

Perhaps it's more challenging to see similar shifts to operating model dynamics in your business, but conditions are in motion right now. In Chapter 2 we discussed how to know when it's time to change through identification of relevant cues from customers, team members, competitors, technology, and economic shifts.

Forty-four years ago, Harvard Business School strategy professor Michael Porter wrote about how competitive forces shape strategy[2]. Porter discussed five competitive forces that define the attractiveness (relative competitiveness) of an industry: the threat of substitute products or services, threat of established rivals, threat of new entrants (contextualized with barriers to entry), bargaining power of suppliers, and bargaining power of customers. Prevailing wisdom says when barriers to entry are low in an industry, the risk of new companies venturing into a given market is high. Conversely, when barriers to entry are high (e.g. significant capital requirements to participate in the industry), incumbents have an advantage over new entrants.

Today, industry disruption is aided by technology and new approaches to innovation, which recalibrate these competitive forces. Most industries - including those once perceived to present high barriers to entry - are vulnerable to disruption. Innovators reduce time-to-market, elevating the threat of substitute offerings. In many industries, the hurdles of high upfront capital requirements no longer exist. E-commerce

---

[2] https://hbr.org/1979/03/how-competitive-forces-shape-strategy

redefined the bargaining power of suppliers and customers and opened the door to a plethora of new business models.

The Tower Records story highlights dynamics in the retail music sales business beginning in 1960. Now, let's explore the manufacturing side of the industry.

The first-generation operating model for recording music dates to 1877, with Thomas Edison's invention of the phonograph. Early recording equipment captured sound on tin foil cylinders. Recording took place outdoors, in home workshops, or hotel rooms. Over the next two decades, technology advanced from Edison's initial inventions to disc-based gramophone and magnetic tape-recording devices.

As tools of the trade developed, professional recording studios designed to capture and transform sound evolved. By the 1950s, studios had become cutting edge, high-tech environments with the development of innovative recording techniques like multi-track recording and tape loops augmenting musical artists' creativity.

To advance and apply these technological developments, record companies and related businesses invested millions of dollars on acoustic design for sound studios, recording equipment and professional talent to engineer recordings. Studios like Abbey Road in London, Capitol Records in Los Angeles, and RCA Studios in Nashville became industry leaders, hosting iconic artists like The Beatles, Frank Sinatra, and Elvis Presley.

Further in the value chain, record producers worked with manufacturing firms, which required large capital investments in pressing and packaging equipment, physical distribution channels, and marketing resources.

The business model evolved to the point that due to high production costs, record companies would only invest in artists with a strong sales history. The cost-benefit of taking on new artists was so great that it limited exposure to new music from independent musicians.

The model was successful and effective until it wasn't. In the 1980s, digital recording technology came of age. Digital audio workstations replaced analog tape machines, enabling greater flexibility, editing capabilities, and affordability. In 1991, Pro Tools, an easy to use, low capital investment (originally around $6,000) digital workstation entered the market and transformed the recording process. Pro Tools enabled new, independent artists (not yet signed with a record label), to record their original music at home with studio-comparable quality.

Technology evolution, combined with the ability to distribute music through streaming platforms like Spotify or SoundCloud and to market through social media is the foundation for an operating model where indie artists can compete with established musicians operating under a stale business model. Artists can create and distribute their product direct to their audience, bypassing the legacy record company operating model.

When has a business model outlived its shelf life? When it no longer advances the organization in the direction of its vision. Identifying cues that conditions are in motion prepares leaders to take preemptive steps in model refinement before it loses relevance.

What is a Business Operating Model?

In the previous chapter, we focused on knowing *when* its time to change. In this chapter, the topic is *what* to change.

A firm's business model (aka: go-to-market model or business operating model) is the way the company goes to market. Business model and strategy are not synonymous. The business model shows how strategy is operationalized to serve customers in context of the macro environment. A business model describes *how* each piece of a business fits together to serve clients. The business model is fulfilment of strategy, which is distilled from demand, supply, and the competitive environment. Strategy guides development of the operating model.

The business operating model looks at each key component, process, and resource necessary to create the desired outcomes. It serves as a playbook for how the business operates, guiding decision-making and ensuring team members alignment with the organization's vision.

Each industry and business are unique. Still there are common characteristics of a business operating model:

- **Target Customers and Specific Segments** (covered in detail in the Which Niche chapter) – Who the business serves (through inference, this also describes out-of-target customers), what the customer values, and what they will pay for. The more specific, the better.
- **Customer Engagement Approach** – How the organization connects to deliver its value proposition to its customers. Business-to-business, business-to-consumer, business-to-business-to-consumer, high touch, high tech, digital only.
- **Value Proposition** – Answers the customer's question: why should I choose your offering? Describes how the business differentiates itself from competitors.
- **Activities and Process Design** – Defines core activities and processes necessary to deliver the value proposition and how they will be performed (i.e. what are the organization's core

competencies and which activities are better left to other firms, what will be produced in-house vs. outsourced or partner-supplied, what are optimal process workflows for efficiency and effectiveness).

- **Resources** - Defines essential resources required to operate the business, including capital, technology, physical assets, partnerships, and vendors.
- **Economic Model** – Describes costs associated with operating the business and informs marketplace positioning (i.e. low-cost leader, premium offering) and pricing strategy.
- **Talent Approach** – Are team members continually developed, effectively coached, properly managed, and thoroughly engaged? Does the company take a different approach to its employees?

Business Model Management

Some firms operate intentionally designed, consistently executed go-to-market business models. Others evolve models in a less structured manner. Regardless of genesis, changes across any of these seven characteristics suggest the need to review and refine a company's business operating model.

The *Leading from Now* approach to business model development is seven steps:

- **Affirm the organization's definition of success (the company's vision)** – An organization's vision is relatively stable, rarely changing. In a review of a company's business model, it's essential to ask: Has our definition of success changed, and if so, how? Significant gaps between an existing vision and the business operating model suggests the company experienced scope creep or the vision needs refinement to reflect the focus of activities.

- **Affirm the organization's culture pillars** - Culture is the shared set of values, beliefs, and behaviors that characterize an organization and influence how its members interact with each other and their stakeholders. Pillars are those foundational descriptors describing the culture like integrity, teamwork, diversity and inclusion, customer centricity, and contribution to the greater good. Clearly defined and documented culture pillars help transmit and reinforce values aligned with vision.

- **Establish organizational priorities aligned with achieving the vision** – This short list of themes governs allocation of resources, time, and energy. As leaders consider establishing a priority, a first question is: How would this priority help advance our organization towards the vision? By ranking priorities high, medium, or low alignment with the stated vision, leaders can focus their resources where they will experience the greatest return. Conversely, if a proposed activity is outside the priorities, leaders must question investing and pay attention to it.

- **Distill priority-linked strategies** - Each priority is operationalized with specific strategies. By building strategies in support of priorities that fulfil the vision, the company's daily activities are efficient.

- **Define and document refined operating model** - Includes specifics about Target Customers and Specific Segments, Customer Engagement Approach, Value Proposition, Activities and Process Design, Resources, Economic Model and Talent Approach.

- **Implement refined operating model** – Each element of the new operating model is allocated to the appropriate team or individual and distilled into individual performance expectations and metrics.
- **Facilitate ongoing change leadership** – Change leadership is not a stand-alone activity, rather it is simply a characteristic of leadership. As an element of business model development, this step can lead back to the first – Affirm the organization's vision as new change stimuli emerge.

Like managing any other organizational asset, business model management is an ongoing process requiring leaders' time and attention. When approached as a business-as-usual endeavor, all participants in the process are better positioned to navigate perpetual motion in the business operating environment.

Value of Self-Initiated Business Model Disruption

Abraham Lincoln is quoted as saying *"Things may come to those who wait, but only the things left by those who hustle."* Translated for business, this message may be interpreted to mean leaders can either act preemptively or reactively. If only the decision was so simple.

Recently, I watched a series of fintech startup investor presentations. These early-stage companies sought venture capital funding to take their ideas to the next level of commerce. By the fifth presentation, I heard the term "disruption" so many times, it sounded like an obligatory disclaimer: "Our goal is to disrupt the [fill-in-the-blank] industry." One could interpret the term as though it is a strategy in-and-of-itself; it is not.

It's easy to think of rapidly changing business environments as those driven by technological development (like the fintech disruptors I observed) and new market entrants. But dynamic conditions are present in most areas of business. A recent article in Funeral Director Daily[3] read, "As our environment continues to experience frequent change, safeguarding your business by remaining vigilant and adapting to the world around you is becoming increasingly important. Funeral Homes are now having to contend with an unpredictable economic climate, regular staff shortages and quickly changing consumer needs. Digitalization is also becoming a bigger part of the industry; digital guests are interacting with services in unique but impactful ways. Those who remain flexible unlock unique opportunities while avoiding the potential hardships that come with inactivity." No business or business model is immune to rapidly changing operating conditions, not even the funeral business.

Disruption happens. It's a natural force as industries evolve. John F. Kennedy said, "Change is the law of life. And those who look only to the past or present are certain to miss the future." Today, innovators capitalize on change to address evolving customer needs, interests, and preferences, and at the same time, many businesses let change take them by surprise.

Knowing the dynamic nature of business and the continuous redefinition of "normal," leaders have a decision to make - initiate change and innovation or react to external pressures forcing adjustment. The most effective leaders proactively look for every opportunity to preemptively refine business operating

---

[3] https://funeraldirectordaily.com/adapting-to-change-in-2023/

models and processes, increase efficiency and improve products and services to their customers.

By practicing self-initiated disruption, leaders proactively identify opportunities to create a business model shift for the benefit of their organization's stakeholders. Austrian economist Joseph Schumpeter used the term "creative destruction" to describe the way free markets evolve. Drawing from Schumpeter's words, self-initiated disruption revolutionizes an organization's value product (what it produces) from within, destroying the old one in favor of a new, more impactful value product.

Self-initiated business model disruption serves two purposes. First, it preempts external disruption by existing competitors and new entrants to your business. Second, it grounds the organization in its reason for existing through the employees, customers and stakeholders served.

Self-initiated disruption is an intentional strategy. Identification of opportunities for self-initiated disruption is a powerful tool for sustaining relevance through business model refinement and redesign.

Change is happening in your business right now. Why not step into *change leadership* through preemptive, self-initiated disruption and define the next iteration of your company's business operating model beginning today?

Defining Problems vs. Delivering Strategy

Business leaders often fall into the trap of believing that if they can eliminate the company's problems, everything will be fine. They get mired in issue identification to the detriment of understanding how the operating environment changes and what those changes mean to their organization. More to the point, the tendency to overemphasize defining problems distracts attention from meaningful, actionable strategy work leading to business model refinement.

Strategic management is an ongoing, dynamic process, comprised of *Leading from Now* for today, tomorrow, and beyond. Today's issues need resolution. The question is: How does the issue de jour become a benefit to our business? When contextualized relative to the company's long-term vision, issues can become connection points between today's actions (including problem resolution) and tomorrow's results.

How can leaders use business issues as strategic building blocks to move their organizations forward? Here are four pivots to help move a business from defining problems to strategic management:

Pivot 1: From eliminating pain points to a strategic management mindset

I recently worked with a bank CEO to organize a strategic planning session with his leadership team. When I asked what success looked like for the session, he held up his list of the top 10 pain points his managers want to resolve. For him, at first blush, success was fixing things that caused his team and customers' pain.

Focusing on removing pain points is a common but misplaced focus. There is nothing wrong with fixing things, but removing pain only gets the business to pain-free, not success. Success means performing activities aligned with the company's vision — moving toward something intentionally defined, not away from something that doesn't work.

The clearer a company is about what it is moving toward, the more successful it will be in executing its strategy. No successful company has a vision of simply being pain-free. There's more to success than the absence of issues. However, used properly, problems (or pain points) can bring clarity to a business's definition of success.

Pivot 2: From description to root cause

Businesspeople often dwell on describing problems in detail, followed by exhaustive analysis. Understanding a problem becomes relevant when leaders go beyond definition to root cause.

By getting to the root cause of an issue (disappointing financial results, declining employee engagement measures, or customer departures as examples), the problem can inform a pivot to the right set of actions that will create the desired outcomes.

Earning, re-earning, and sustaining relevance with stakeholders is a daily endeavor which requires a clear understanding of operating results - why a strategy works or falls short of producing expected outcomes. Deconstructing results and finding the root cause simply means understanding the set of activities and circumstances that created outcomes, then adjusting accordingly for different results.

Understanding the root cause leads to greater awareness and new ideas to fulfill the organization's vision.

Pivot 3: From struggle to strength

An effective business strategy emphasizes attention to core competencies - things a company does best - and steers clear of anything outside that nucleus. This means leaders must be honest with themselves and their organization about what their company does well and what would be better left to others.

Struggle is often an effect of engaging in activities, projects, or strategies that do not play to the company's strengths. There is tremendous power in knowing what your company doesn't do well or shouldn't do at all. When a business is clear in its future-state vision, it's easier to know which activities, decisions, hiring choices, or partnerships align - and which are out of scope.

Having this clarity helps avoid wasting time on activities that will never be a good fit with the business operating model. This applies to the daily activities a business invests its time in, as well as bigger-picture endeavors like joint ventures or mergers and acquisitions.

In-N-Out Burger[4] is a terrific example of playing to strengths. They make burgers, fries, and shakes. No chicken sandwiches. No turkey sandwiches. No salads. They do burgers, fries, and shakes exceptionally well (in the view of their customers, which is what counts).

Pivot 4: From issue identification to refined business model

There is power in problems when leaders leverage learnings from issue assessment to evolve a new business operating model. Business model longevity is defined by many variables described in this book. The sooner cues and clues which suggest it's time for a model refresh are examined, the better positioned the organization to advance toward its vision.

Back to New Year's Eve three years from now, and the self-imposed question: *What did I do as a leader that had the greatest impact on my business in over the past year?* One powerful answer can be, "Over the summer, I reviewed our company's business operating model and see how it aligns with the future we

---

[4] https://digitalsparkmarketing.com/competitive-strategy/

anticipate. The changes we made later that year led to a breakout performance and outstanding results!"

Chapter 4
The Most Common Business Model Issues

It depends. I'm not sure exactly what it depends on, but I know – it depends. I'm referring to pizza. Homemade is my favorite, but when that's not an option and my wife and I don't want to go out for dinner, I'm happy to order home delivery pizza.

We usually order pizza from a local franchisee of a national chain. One Friday evening, Norma delivered our pizza. About half the time, she not only takes our phone order, but she makes the pizza and delivers it. On this particular night, Norma did it all – took our order, made the pizza, then delivered it.

When I saw her pull up in front of our house, I went out to the curb to meet her. Norma handed me the pizza, I thanked her, then turned around to go inside. As I headed back into the house, a neighbor passed by. She saw me carrying the pizza boxes and asked, "How do you like this pizza brand?"

I felt the urge to respond immediately and say, "Norma is terrific, and she makes great pizzas." But I paused for a millisecond and thought - when Norma doesn't make the pizza, the product is inconsistent. Sometimes it's good; other times, it's not good at all. Not enough sauce, too little cheese, burned crust. My answer to the neighbor: "It depends."

I learned later (from Norma) that the pizza store has one process to fulfill online orders. Phone orders are handled differently, and walk-in orders receive a third approach. What does the customer get? It depends.

In contrast, Forklore Restaurant Group (pseudonym for an actual restaurant chain) is unwilling to accept "It depends" as a customer experience option. Forklore operates upscale restaurants under more than a dozen different brand names through a consistent business model. In the late 1970s, Forklore's founders set out to establish an upscale restaurant that combined consistency and quality in a manner not previously delivered in full-service restaurants. Forklore's commitment to create a consistent, repeatable dining experience was measured against a set of high standards and attention to details.

My introduction to Forklore Restaurant Group was through a restaurateur and founder of another large restaurant chain.

I asked, "When you're not eating at one of your restaurants, what is your favorite place to dine?"

He said, "Forklore in Newport Beach."

I asked, "Why?"

He said, "Consistency and quality."

Subsequently, I learned that Forklore restaurants train employees to deliver a consistent, engaging customer experience. Each step – from initial guest greeting, through delivery of first round beverages within two minutes of seating, how orders are taken, presentation of food for optimal aesthetics, check delivery, and everything in between – is thoroughly choreographed. Activities in the kitchen follow an equally well-defined operating model to assure food quality consistency. And managers ensure consistent, end-to-end execution of the operating model.

Most restaurants want consistency for the guests. Forklore Restaurant Group deploys a business operating model that assures this.

When the answer is - It depends - there may be a business model issue at play. Evidence from the pizza store example suggests at least three different operating models, defined by ordering channel (phone, online, in-store), each with a different outcome. This is one of many common go-to-market business operating model issues.

Think about your experience as a customer or even as an employee of an organization with a poorly designed business model or no intentional model at all. When the answer is "It depends," outcomes are unpredictable, and as a result, business is at risk. In this chapter, we cover some of the most common business model issues.

No Clear Go to Market Model

Sometimes businesses grow out of a successful product or service. There is demand for the offering, which provides the producer with an initial engagement approach with the customer. In the software arena, a similar concept is the Minimum Viable Product which describes the basic version of a product with the minimum features needed to meet user needs. However, a product or service on its own is not a go to market business model.

When a well-defined go to market model has not been developed, or the model exists but is outdated, a company is likely to experience below average growth, increasing customer attrition, and economic challenges over time.

Recommended Action: Follow the *Leading from Now* seven step approach to business model development described in Chapter 3 to formalize a go-to-market model for your company or to assess an existing model you suspect may be outdated.

Unclear or Undeveloped Playbook

Imagine attending a Broadway musical which had no script, no choreography, no blocking. Actors are left to their own creativity to tell the story, develop, and deliver their lines, sing their songs, and interact with other performers. Odds are the audience would see confusion, disorganization, or chaos on stage.

In contrast, Broadway plays generally have thoroughly developed scripts, performed by highly trained actors who have memorized their lines, learned the choreography, and know exactly how to engage with their colleagues on stage.

When a firm has not developed a playbook for serving customers, the result can look like the play without a script. Leaders and staff do their best to deliver to customers, but performances are improvised and inconsistent.

A well-defined playbook serves as a roadmap that outlines the firm's approach to customer engagement. Team choreography and the client experience are defined, roles and responsibilities are clear, and management can focus on consistent execution.

Recommended Action: After defining your business model, develop a playbook to describe roles, responsibilities, and outcomes for your business. Rather than a document for occasional reference, this playbook becomes the roadmap for all team members.

Lack of a Clearly Defined Target Customer or Specific Segments

Who is our customer? A simple question that often goes unanswered or is answered in a manner incongruent with the business. Yet, failure to define your customer can have significant economic and resource allocation implications.

I worked with a wealth management firm that had 9,500 accounts for 4,000 clients (most clients have multiple accounts). Our engagement focused on the identification of opportunities to accelerate growth. Through our discovery and assessment process, we learned staffing was the top growth constraint.

On further analysis, a more profound issue arose. While the company had a stated minimum relationship size of $500,000 (value of all assets managed for a client across accounts), the actual average relationship size was below $200,000. That meant a business model designed for larger relationships – defined as clients with at least $500,000 managed by the firm – overloaded its resources. It takes two and a half $200,000 relationships to equal one $500,000 relationship. A staffing model developed to handle larger relationships was choked with more than twice the volume people were prepared to service.

The solution to this firm's business model issue was two-fold – re-establish clarity about their target client and develop a segmentation strategy to effectively serve existing smaller relationships. Through this exercise, the firm increased its minimum new relationship size to $1 million in managed assets.

Recommended Action: Define your business's target customer. Your target customer should be one you can serve exceptionally well, drawing from the company's core competencies. If your customer base is large, explore segmentation and provide differentiated offerings in each segment served as economically warranted.

Inconsistent or Poorly Defined Customer Experience (aka Customer Engagement)

"If you don't know where you are going, any road can take you there." Those words from *Alice in Wonderland*'s Cheshire Cat work in a children's storybook. Lacking a clear destination in the customer journey doesn't work so well.

When each employee is left to find their own way in creating a customer experience, inconsistent delivery is the result. Unintentionally, customers receive varying levels of service across touchpoints from initial engagement through sale, product (service) usage and ongoing support.

Common factors that contribute to an inconsistent customer experience include:

- No clear answer to the question: What does a customer get when they choose our offering?
- Lack of standardized processes – e.g., customer engagement approach, sales process, product (service) delivery, ongoing support, proactive customer outreach.
- Communication gaps – Inconsistent, ineffective, or insufficient communications, lack of proactive customer outreach, slow response times to customer inquiries.
- Failure to understand customer preferences – Assuming one size (or communication style) fits all customers overlooks individual differences in information preferences, learning styles, and interests.
- Inadequate employee training and development – Training on the firm's customer experience model (like with the Folklore Restaurant Group), and all aspects of guiding the customer journey is a necessary foundation for delivering a consistent experience.

Recommended Action: Document today's customer journey, then compare the experience with your company's vision. When you identify gaps, use learnings to develop and implement a future state customer journey map.

Unclear or Missing Value Proposition, Failure to Articulate "Why me, why us."

One of the most common questions on the minds of prospective customers is, "Why should I do business with you and your company?" Failure to articulate "why me, why our firm" leaves it up to the prospect to define your value proposition, contributing to a business model issue. Companies and customer-facing employees who cannot answer these questions clearly, succinctly, and deliver on their value proposition are likely to underperform.

Research tells us that the decision process for selecting a service business provider (accountant, attorney, banker, consultant, medical professional) is multifaceted, and includes who the customer-facing individual is (background, experience, similar clients), reputation of the firm, trustworthiness of the individual and firm, nature of the offering, value, and perceptions of the individual service provider's ability to consistently deliver.

We also know that relevance as a product or service provider – meaningfulness, pertinence, and importance – must continually be re-earned. Doing a great job yesterday only matters until a new day begins. Therefore, having and communicating a clear value proposition helps contextualize a company's relevance to a customer.

Recommended Action: With clarity about your business's target customer, a company can articulate its value proposition. To experience the greatest benefit, the value proposition must be well understood, co-owned, and applied by all employees. This will require training, coaching and ongoing oversight by management.

Activities and Process Design

In a perfect world, activities within an organization are synchronized into processes which align with a clearly defined vision. In reality, many companies perform organizational activities independent of a specific purpose (like fulfilling the company's vision) or are misaligned with success metrics. More activities that do not align with vision fulfillment means resources (human and all other categories) are distracted from advancing the organization.

Activities are building blocks for processes which support other processes across an organization. While precision functions – product assembly, manufacturing, surgery, piloting an airplane – require a well-documented, consistently repeatable series of steps, many business processes are not formalized. However, lack of formal documentation in no way negates the existence of a process. These informal processes can be observed, defined, re-engineered, or discontinued.

Drawbacks to informal processes are inconsistency in performance of activities, overload of information required to properly perform activities, challenges identifying root cause of issues, efficiency limitations, and business model breakdowns.

Banking is a heavily regulated industry and satisfying regulatory requirements is non-negotiable. Yet, a common misperception - *policies and procedures are the same* - produces unnecessary inefficiencies in the way traditional banks serve customers. How does this happen? Banking regulations emanate from legislation or through a regulatory agency proclamation, the Office of the Comptroller of the Currency for example. New regulations are disseminated to banks for interpretation through their compliance department. Bank compliance departments then distill each regulation into a policy to be followed by bank employees.

Bank regulations impact consumers directly or indirectly, yet it is rare for a bank to define, design and deliver a customer-based process for policy (therefore, regulation) implementation. Banks often lose sight of the intent of a regulation, and by default apply the rule as a process itself. Paradoxically, it is rare for a regulation to *define* a process. Banking regulators generally describe an expected outcome with a new regulation but leave process design to each bank. In this flexibility resides an opportunity for banks to design interoperable processes which satisfy regulators and address existing and emerging customer needs, thereby strengthening their business operating model.

By intentionally framing activities in a process context, leaders reduce risks resulting from individual differences in selecting activities to perform, decrease the likelihood of employees overlooking necessary steps for successful task completion, and create a structure for business model success.

Recommended Action: Vision distils into priorities, strategies, and activities. Work toward synchronizing organizational activities into processes which align with a clearly defined vision. Assess each strategy for alignment with the vision.

Resources

Each business operating model is a recipe for how companies go to market. The necessary resources are required ingredients to operate the business, including human, intellectual and financial capital, technology, physical assets, partnerships, and vendors.

Issues arise when resources misalign with a company's intentionally defined business model. An early stage fintech firm deployed a go-to-market model built around an app-based financial planning tool. The company promoted the availability of financial planning professionals to answer questions for the do-it-yourself customers who needed some assistance (a majority of their customer base). However, they didn't invest in sufficient staffing for the customer support service. The outcome was negative online reviews and feedback from frustrated users, which damaged the brand. They eventually expanded support service resources, but rebuilding the company's reputation took years.

Recommended Action: Evaluate your company's resource allocation with its vision. The annual budget is a good proxy for asset allocation. How do budgeted expenses align with the vision? Where do adjustments need to be made for optimal alignment?

Economic Model

With similarities to Resources, the Economic model describes costs and scale associated with operating the business relative to the business model and revenue opportunities, and informs marketplace positioning (i.e. low-cost leader, premium offering) and pricing strategy. When a business model is at odds with a company's economics, profit margins are an early indicator of issues.

A small independent pharmacy opened across the street from a large hospital and medical center in the city where I live, . It was started by a pharmacist who promoted competitive prices, large inventory, fast prescription preparation time and friendly service. As an independent, the pharmacist didn't have the scale, purchasing power or technology of her competitors, making it difficult for the business model to succeed.

CVS, with 25% share of the market nationally, was located at the intersection. Walmart (4% share), Ralphs/Kroger (3% share), Rite Aid (2% share), Albertsons (1% share), and Costco (.6% share) were all located within three miles of this pharmacy. Her economic model was incongruent with the business model, causing the pharmacy to fail in less than six months.

For most types of business, a low-priced provider business model requires high volume, economies of scale, and large scope. Lower volume operations are more likely to succeed though a model built upon differentiation (more on this in the Which Niche chapter).

Recommended Action: Assess your company's economic model in the context of your target customer, scope, and scale of production. Identify and address gaps between the business and economic models.

Talent Approach

Even in the AI era, it is understood that people are essential to the organization. And it's common for companies to include the importance of their team members in their stated values. The business model breakdown occurs when a disconnect between the stated (or expected) and experienced approach to talent management occurs. When a company's business model calls for highly trained customer service professionals, then fails to provide ongoing staff training, the model is at risk.

Sweetwater is an online musical equipment retailer headquartered in Fort Wayne, Indiana. Founded in 1979,

Sweetwater's business model calls for offering "quality instruments and music equipment, expert service, and amazing support"...everything music makers need and more.

Sweetwater customer service representatives are called sales engineers. The company's website says, "These industry insiders don't just sell music gear; they also work with you to come up with smart solutions to your unique challenges. Whether you need an amp rig for your next transatlantic tour or a simple recording setup that fits your budget, you can count on these highly qualified experts." Sounds great, but how does the company support this business model?

I spoke with Jon, a five-year Sweetwater sales engineer. He explained that as a new employee, all Sweetwater sales engineers receive detailed product training through Sweetwater University (an in-house learning and development resource) across the complete product catalog before engaging directly with customers. Once a sales engineer is on the line, they receive regular new product briefings and ongoing product and technical training. In addition, sales engineers get regular performance feedback from their manager.

Sweetwater sales engineers must have a specialization – guitars, basses, keyboards, mixing, recording and sound equipment, and in most cases, are music makers themselves. Jon is a guitar specialist and plays the instrument. As a guitarist myself, I asked Jon several general and specific guitar questions, and he had answers.

Next, I asked Jon about guitar pedals – sound effects and tone enhancements used by electric guitar players.

Jon said, "I can talk with you about effect pedals, but I have a teammate who specializes in that area. Can I have him join the call to get into details of what you're looking for?"

After speaking with Jon and his colleague, they sent me a YouTube link to a video by Don. Don is a professional guitarist who provides product demos, reviews, how-to's, and group instruction for Sweetwater customers. Sweetwater is an exemplary example of a company that aligns its talent approach with its business model.

The chapter entitled *How People Development Makes a Company More Competitive* addresses this topic in more detail.

Recommended Action: Assess your company's business model requirements of its employees. Ask: how do we know employees are properly prepared for their continually evolving roles? Are team members continually developed, effectively coached, properly managed, and thoroughly engaged? Then develop and implement steps to address all gaps.

Fragmentation

It depends. This chapter began with the pizza franchisee case. Three different pizza experiences based on how a customer's order is placed - one approach to fulfill online orders, a second for phone orders, and a third process for walk-in orders. This is business model fragmentation.

There are times companies appear to think, "It's all about us." Employees operate independently, with different objectives, goals, incentives, and customer experience definitions. What's wrong with this picture? Losing sight of what should matter most: the customer. The root cause is lack of clarity about who the company serves and how they serve them.

In contrast, when a firm's go-to-market operating model starts with the customer, and a clearly defined customer experience roadmap, the dynamic changes. When each person involved in creating the customer experience knows the definition of success, and their individual role in its creation, the company delivers a much stronger performance. A fragmented approach to understanding and addressing customer needs reflects a self-centeredness of the firm vs. what customers deem important.

Recommended Action: De-fragmentation requires an intentionally designed go-to-market business model built around the customer. Review how your company delivers on its offering with an eye for signs of fragmentation or inconsistency. From there, develop and implement a plan to assure consistent delivery of the desired customer experience.

Chapter 5
Leading Change

As much as I try, I'm not great at picking gifts for people. I consider myself creative, but when it comes to gift ideas for family and friends, it's a challenge for me. On the other hand, my wife and kids excel as creative gift givers. For my birthday, my son took me to the Porsche Driving Experience in Los Angeles. I love cars, especially German sports cars, making this a perfect gift.

My session included a performance driving coach and 90 minutes behind the wheel of two different Porsche cars – the electric Taycan Turbo and a 640 horsepower 911 Turbo. With in-depth guidance from my coach, I raced a 1.3-mile handling course, designed to emulate a canyon road, with tight corners and long straightaways, an ice hill that simulates slippery mountain conditions, and a kick-plate which causes loss of vehicle control so drivers can learn to navigate unexpected conditions.

As part of the performance driving training, my coach said, "The two things that matter most in driving through expected and unanticipated conditions are vision and alignment. Keep your focus on where you're going, then make sure your steering and pedal control align." The same can be said for leading change: Two things that matter most are vision (success defined) and alignment (how the organization manifests its vision)!

Change Leadership

Change Leadership refers to proactive, ongoing adaptation of an organization to its operating environment, which is in perpetual motion. Change Leadership, as an element of strategic management, is an ongoing, dynamic process. Why? Operating conditions are in perpetual motion. Leaders must be attuned to conditions in the present moment to infer and inform actions taken today, aligned with future state success.

Leaders have a choice: intentionally initiate adaptive organizational change or react to forces which *will* evolve the business. Vision sets the course, then informs actions defined by the business operating model. In the words of my performance driving coach, vision, and alignment (with the business model) are the foundation of effective change leadership.

An important distinction is the difference between *change leadership* as an element of every leader's responsibility and *change management* endeavors. The principle: operating conditions are in perpetual motion, thus navigating change is simply business as usual. In contrast, *change management* projects are events with a beginning, middle and an end. Most often, change management efforts are a reaction to something like changes in customers expectations, and the competitive, economic, technological, regulatory, or resource environment.

Change Leadership Tools

As a student of strategic management in graduate school, I learned four conversation starter questions for business leaders: Where are we now? (with our business), Where are we going? (aka: the vision), How will we get there? (the business operating model), and Where can we anticipate changes along the journey? The traditional SWOT analysis guides leaders in answering the first two questions but doesn't address questions three and four. The SWOT analysis captures existing strengths, weaknesses, opportunities, and threats, but falls short on incorporating future changes in customers, employees, technology, competition, and the overall operating environment.

The **Change Leadership Opportunity Assessment** (CLOA) was developed to guide leaders in evaluating leading and lagging indicators of the need to initiate business model changes. The CLOA's leading indicators are forward looking signals suggesting future trends or outcomes. They aim to identify seeds of change before they become fully evident. Leading indicators are like the headlights on a car, illuminating the road ahead. Lagging indicators confirm trends that have already begun. Lagging indicators are like a car's rearview mirror, showing us where we've been.

Leading indicators suggesting the need to initiate business model changes include:

- Signals of changing customer mix or preferences
- Observed changes in customer or employee satisfaction or engagement
- Emerging technologies
- Changes in employee engagement
- New competitors
- New products
- Increased complaints
- Unfavorable online and social media traffic
- Pricing deterioration

The CLOA's lagging indicators include:

- Evidence of shifting demand
- Evidence of increasing supply of offerings like your company's
- Increases in customer attrition
- Increases in employee attrition
- Changes in the job applicant pool

- Increases in employee attrition
- Decline in repeat customers
- Increases in product returns
- Fewer new customers
- Decreasing average sales
- Margin deterioration

Change Leadership Opportunity Assessment	
Leading Indicators	Lagging Indicators (Reactive Change)
Indicators of changing customer preferences	Evidence of shifting demand
Observed changes in customer satisfaction or engagement	Evidence of increasing supply of offerings like your company's
Emerging technologies targeting all or part of your company's value proposition	Increasing regrettable employee attrition
Observed changes in employee engagement or satisfaction	Changes in size, qualifications of job applicant pool for open positions
Entry of new competitors to your market	Increasing customer attrition
Exit of existing competitors from your market	Decline in repeat customers
New products offered by competitors	Fewer new customers
Increased customer complaints	Decreasing average sales per customer
Unfavorable online and social media traffic	Margin deterioration
Pricing deterioration	Increasing product returns

Each indicator is intended to focus leaders' attention on factors likely to necessitate a business model change. Early detection of changing conditions allows leaders time to explore strategic alternatives, which may not be available to the company over time.

The CLOA augments a traditional SWOT analysis by introducing dynamic elements of a business's operating environment. No single indicator (including the SWOT analysis) provides a complete picture. Using a combination of leading and lagging indicators, along with other data and analysis, prepares leaders to know when it's time for proactive change.

The Change Guidance Framework provides leaders with questions in seven areas of focus critical in navigating change. It begins with an inquiry into the future state picture and the organization's vision (what does success look like?). The Framework includes questions about co-ownership of the organization's vision, the roadmap from where the business is today, and its destination. Effective communications are core to every organization, so the Framework delves into the nature, content, and frequency of information flow. Navigating change always includes barriers to progress. The Framework encourages leaders to anticipate and prepare for inevitable barriers. As change leadership is an ongoing process, I include questions regarding sustainability. Finally, an organization's stakeholders need effective channels for feedback regarding how the business is showing up. Feedback Loop questions encourage leaders to actively seek and measure progress and perceptions from their constituents.

Focus	Questions
Future State Picture	• What does success look like for this program? For the business overall? • How does the future state picture (vision) compare with the current environment? • What about the future state vision is compelling? Concerning? How will our future state vision focus, guide daily activities?
Co-ownership	• What role will team members play in defining the future state picture? • How do we assure broad co-ownership of our future state vision? • Which stakeholder group's buy-in is essential? Important? Beneficial? • What is our engagement governance approach?
Roadmap	• What are the specific areas of focus and activities to bridge the gap between the current environment and future state vision? • What are the workstreams necessary to address each area of focus? • How will we adjust the roadmap as conditions evolve?
Communication	• Who are our different audiences and how do communication needs differ for each group? • How will we approach initial program communication and messaging?

	• How will we approach ongoing program updates, progress and challenges throughout the journey? • What is the right frequency of communication?
Navigating Barriers	• What and where are anticipated barriers to advancing this program and how will we address them? • Where are known points of resistance to this program and how will we address them? • What is our governance approach to addressing unanticipated barriers and points of resistance?
Assuring Sustainability	• How will we ensure regular reengagement of the organization in fulfilling the future state vision? • How will we recognize and reward actions that advance the future state vision? • How will we address actions that do not align with advancing the future state vision? • How often will we meet as leaders to sustain engagement?
Feedback Loop	• What OKRs or deliverables will we measure and report on? • How will we elicit and assess stakeholder feedback throughout this program? • What mechanisms will we use to gather and share stakeholder feedback?

Why is Organizational Change a Challenge?

Mark Twain said, "The only person who likes change is a baby with a wet diaper." Twain may be right, yet navigating change is essential for effective leadership. Still, most human beings have a natural resistance to change.

Change often involves disruption to the status quo. In its current usages, the term status quo means keeping things the same. However, the meaning has evolved over time. This Latin term translates to "the state in which things are." It was originally used in legal contexts to refer to the existing state of things that both parties agreed to maintain. Over time, the term broadened to describe the current situation in any context (not just legal or political). Noteworthy is that the original meaning did not imply steady state (not subject to change), rather simply the current state of conditions.

We are attracted to the stability of steady state conditions. Comfort anchored in conditions can only last if conditions are static. As conditions evolve (which is constant), a new normal is born. Still, "Status quo" is a Latin phrase that means "existing state of affairs."

In 1988, researchers William Samuelson and Richard Zeckhauser introduced the concept of Status Quo Bias - the preference for maintaining one's current situation and opposing actions that may change that situation. Status quo bias is a cognitive bias based on emotion.

Samuelson and Zeckhauser's academic article "Status Quo Bias in Decision-Making"[5] discussed a series of decision-making experiments. This research found that when given a choice between the status quo and a new option, individuals were more likely to stick with what they already knew. This bias negatively affects our ability to make decisions. Our desire for a steady state may prevent us from evaluating emerging options objectively, leading to missed opportunities and elevated risk due to inaction. Status quo bias can have a deleterious impact on a business when it prevents adaptation as operating conditions evolve.

Comfort in current conditions blends with fear of the unknown, comfort with the status quo, lack of understanding of the reasons behind impending changes, lack of clarity about what success looks like, or individual behavioral styles. Our brains are wired to seek familiarity and stability. When conditions contradict these anchors, we can feel anxious and apprehensive. It's easy to be emotionally attached to our routines, even when they no longer align with our individual needs.

Then, there is the behavioral science around loss aversion. Humans tend to prioritize avoiding losses over the potential for

---

[5]

https://www.researchgate.net/publication/5152072_Status_Quo_Bias_in_Decision-Making

receiving gains (like the risk aversion dimension of status quo bias). Perceptions about potential losses associated with change - disrupted routines, loss of control, or failure – may outweigh the perceived benefits.

These factors, and individual behavioral styles, like a natural proclivity toward predictability and consistency, can contribute to habitual resistance. Changing habits requires a clear replacement habit, motivation, incentive, and continuous reinforcement.

When we move from individual factors affecting navigating change to those at the organizational level, it's like moving from basic math to multivariate calculus. An organization is simply a community of individuals. What is true at the individual level about change is exponentially amplified at the organizational level.

Change resistance refers to reluctance or opposition of individuals or teams within a firm to embrace and adapt to changes in processes, technologies, strategies, or organizational structure. Collective habits, routines, fears, and cultural characteristics can play into change resistance. At the leadership level of a company, lack of trust in leadership, poor communications, and lack of training and support make resistance to organizational change more challenging.

I worked with an independent bank that recently changed CEOs. They created multiple vision statements, but they weren't what employees could articulate or aspire to. The bank had no clear value proposition (little consistency across the institution about why customers would choose this bank, or their differentiation). Perhaps to no surprise, the business model was fragmented; it was unclear if the bank's focus was business-to-consumer (B2C), business-to-business (B2B), or business-to-business-to-consumer (B2B2C).

After 45 days of deep-dive sessions with leaders, team members, partners, customers, former employees, and board members, we advanced a set of foundational agreements. First, the bank operated as a B2B2C service provider; it only interacted with end-user customers through other businesses. Rather than seeing these other businesses as "internal clients," the bank redefined these relationships as partnerships. Second, given the B2B2C business model, the bank refined their vision, recognizing that their definition of success needed to include value for their partners as well as the end-user customers. Third, a set of five priorities was established and distilled into a strategic roadmap for the bank.

Sidenote: Addressing the vision *after* addressing the business operating model may sound inconsistent with the *vision first* recommendation in previous chapters. In this specific case, the level of confusion experienced following the previous CEO's departure required triage, beginning with clearly answering the question: What business are we in? That line of inquiry led to addressing the business model first, then refining existing vision statements into a single, engaging definition of success for the bank.

The bank's new strategic plan and associated funding was unanimously approved by their board for immediate implementation. The leadership team was pleased with their work, and ready to begin implementation. Then, seemingly out of nowhere, the Groundhog Day scenario began.

Members of the bank's leadership team who were actively engaged in vision development, business model definition and strategic plan detailing suddenly began resisting implementation. In some cases, resistance was direct and blatant – "nobody really believes in this plan," "we've tried all this before, and it won't work," "the board of directors doesn't have a clue about what really happens in our business," or "all of the best people in the bank will leave and go to a better firm as soon as they have a chance." In other cases, resistance was much more nuanced – "our old CEO was on the right track, she just needed more time to move things forward," "things aren't as bad as the board makes it sound; they just need more data," and "I think we need to take the next few months to analyze our business in more depth before we make any changes,"

These reactions and resistance seemed inconsistent with the energy applied to the plan development process. Through in-depth analysis, we learned the stakeholders demonstrating greatest resistance to change were members of the bank's leadership team (the very people that co-created the bank's new roadmap).

To help uncover individual challenges to advancing the bank's new strategic plan, we engaged a DISC Certified Trainer. DISC is a behavioral self-assessment tool developed by psychologist William Moulton Marston, based on his emotional and behavioral theory published in 1928. The DISC assessment is designed to anticipate job performance by categorizing individuals' natural behavioral styles into four characteristics – Dominance (direct, strong-willed, forceful, fast-paced, skeptical), Influence (sociable, talkative, lively, fast-paced and accepting), Steadiness (gentle, accommodating, soft-hearted, cautious, and accepting) and Conscientious (private, analytical, logical, cautious, and skeptical).

DISC profiles for the bank's 22 managers led to an aha moment. Global DISC distribution data indicates 9% of the population has Dominance as their primary style; 29% Influence; 32% Steadiness; and 30% Conscientious. However, at this bank, 90% – 16 of these 18 managers – had a single behavioral style – Conscientious as their top style, followed by Steadiness as the second. This is statistically highly unusual, and important in understanding these leaders' resistance to change.

According to the DISC style descriptions, people with a Conscientious/Steadiness behavioral style highly value stability, minimizing risk, and experiencing reliable, consistent outcomes. They tend to be cautious, reflective, stable, reliable, orderly, careful, and conventional.

Remarkable! Ninety percent of the bank's leaders had individual behavioral styles resistant to change. In aggregate, this amplified common challenges associated with navigating change. The solution for this bank was to create a series of steps to develop agility acumen among its leaders. The program, anchored in the company's vision and values, supported advancement of the new business model.

More details on organizational agility in the next chapter. Meanwhile, the takeaway from this case study for change leaders is this: While there are many factors which contribute to the challenge of change - comfort in current conditions, fear of the unknown, lack of understanding of the reasons supporting changes – the human element, and individual behavioral styles in particular, must be recognized and fully addressed for successful change leadership.

Owning Change Leadership

In the business world, the track record for successful change management is mixed at best. When it comes to navigating change, we know a great deal about what doesn't work:

- Failing to develop a clear picture of the organization's future state.
- Failing to engage people across the organization in co-owning a future-state vision.
- Failing to develop a deliberate roadmap between the current environment and future state.
- Failing to communicate frequently about progress and challenges in the journey.
- Failing to regularly re-engage the organization in the future state vision.
- Failing to adjust the roadmap as conditions evolve.

Even with a well-documented body of knowledge about what doesn't work, there is a dearth of success stories when it comes to change management victories. Still, every organization is faced with navigating a continually changing operating environment.

Five fundamental factors are needed to overcome inertia that stifles change programs – a clear future state vision, engagement, communication, actualization, and reinforcement. Every venture, be it a start-up or an ongoing enterprise, begins with a vision of what success looks like – what an organization wants to demonstrate. From there, engagement with key stakeholders – employees, partners, owners – gives the change endeavor traction and sustainability. Frequent, regular communication with stakeholders about where the organization is going and about progress and accomplishments toward the vision create transparency. Actualization brings specific results to life and highlights progress for the organization to observe. Reinforcement means frequent re-articulation of the vision, the roadmap to fulfil it, and progress.

What can Leaders do to Elevate their Success with Change Leadership?

Recognize it for what it is – Changing conditions can include process redesign, new technology and tools, or a refined go-to-market model. Whatever is included, there is always a behavioral change element to change management. According to Professor Megan Call[6] at the University of Utah, "Behavior change is complicated and complex because it requires a person to disrupt a current habit while simultaneously fostering a new, possibly unfamiliar, set of actions. This process takes time, usually longer than we prefer."

When leaders recognize part of their role (as change leaders) is to invite, support and facilitate behavioral change, it can clarify what's necessary to advance the business and traverse forces that reinforce the status quo.

Act accordingly – When leaders understand the core elements required to stimulate behavioral change, they can align their energy with actions to support team members. Taking steps to (1) align the change effort with a clear description of success, (2) create co-ownership in the change initiative, (3) initiate relevant tasks, behavioral and social communications, (4) earn and sustain engagement in bringing the future-state vision to life will enhance the organization's change acumen.

Identify opportunities for self-initiated disruption– Disruption happens. It's a natural force as industries evolve. John F. Kennedy said, "Change is the law of life. And those who look only to the past or present are certain to miss the future."

---

[6] https://accelerate.uofuhealth.utah.edu/resilience/why-is-behavior-change-so-hard#:~:text=Behavior%20change%20is%20complicated%20and,usually%20longer%20than%20we%20prefer.

Capitalizing on perpetual motion, innovators create industry disruption to address evolving customer needs, interests, and preferences. At the same time, many businesses let change take them by surprise. Knowing the dynamic nature of business, and the continuous redefinition of "normal," leaders have a decision to make—initiate change and innovate or react to external pressures. Self-initiated disruption serves two purposes. First, it preempts external disruption by existing competitors and new entrants to your business. Second, it grounds the organization in its reason for existing through the employees, customers, and stakeholders served.

Integrate preemptive change opportunity identification into regular business operating reviews – Broaden standard quarterly financial performance reviews to include conversations about indicators of changing customer needs, preferences, trends, operational improvement opportunities, new technologies applicable to your business, new vendor practices, and the like. This will identify seeds with the potential to grow into full-blown paradigm shifts for your organization.

Recognize change leadership is part of *leadership* **and own it** – French philosopher, Rene Descartes wrote that if you choose not to decide, you still have made a choice. All leaders need to adjust to a rapidly changing environment, and choosing not to act is rarely a good option. In the context of perpetual change, develop your organization's acumen in *leading change.* Champion a vision of where the organization is going in the evolution of who you serve and how you deliver to your customers and build esprit de corps with agility as a core competency.

Chapter 6
Developing Agility as an Organizational Competency

Imagine that every year, your business replaced its core technology platform. While many processes are similar, the platform is new. The same is true for all your competitors; new technology and new approaches to competing arise every year. In addition, frequent regulatory changes affect the way you operate. Your team members receive some training, but competency development evolves from on-the-job experience throughout the year. Each year your customers change – who they are, what they expect. You need to continually recruit new talent to your team because turnover is a challenge. And the cost of doing business rises. If you have a great year, revenue is strong; if your team's performance is average or lower, economic results will drop.

This describes the business of Formula 1 racing, which has ten F1 teams, each with two race cars, drivers, and employees. The largest team, Mercedes AMG Petronas, has 1,200 employees. Although they are not required to change cars every year, teams generally do so to remain competitive and improve results over the previous year. New cars mean new technology, tools, processes, and learnings. The investment required to participate in F1 racing is significant. In 2023, the per team budget cap stood at $135 million. Driver compensation, excluded from the budget cap, ranges from about $1 million a year to over $60 million in 2022. F1 direct revenue in 2023 was $2.57 billion, driven by in-person event attendance and global viewership. F1 teams generate revenue from prize money (better performance equates to greater revenue), sponsorships, and car manufacturers.

With roots in Grand Prix racing, F1 evolved from European championships of the 1920s with open-wheeled cars like the Mercedes-Benz Silver Arrow. In 1946 the Fédération Internationale de l'Automobile recognized the need for standardization and established and frequently updates F1 regulations, specifying engine sizes, car weights, safety features and race rules.

Success as a Formula 1 racing team requires *organizational agility*, which means leaders and team members:

- Are attuned to continually evolving conditions within their business.
- Monitor subtle, gradual, rapid, or event-driven shifts in the external operating environment.
- Infer implications of environmental dynamics for their business.
- Adapt and adjust activities, resource allocation, and operating models as conditions change.
- Recognize that change leadership is not an overlay to the business; it is the business.

In the 2023 F1 season, driver champion Max Verstappen and the Red Bull Racing Team exemplified agility. Racing conditions – weather, track temperature, track design – vehicle performance, team and driver performance, the competitive landscape and race strategy are in perpetual motion.

At race time, the temperature for the Abu Dhabi Grand Prix was 90 degrees with a light wind blowing across the track. For most of the race, famed Mercedes AMG Petronas driver Lewis Hamilton was in a wheel-to-wheel battle with Max Verstappen, Team Red Bull's rising star. Every curve, pit stop, every strategic gamble resembled a high-stakes soccer game for the ultimate prize - the Formula 1 championship.

With five laps to go, a sudden sandstorm swirled across the racetrack. Suddenly operating conditions changed dramatically, and the strategy had to be reinvented.

Team Mercedes, drawing on robust data analytics, hesitated. Was it time to pull Lewis into the pit for new tires, expecting the sandstorm to subside, or run the remining laps on the existing tires?

Team Red Bull capitalized on changing conditions and evolved their strategy. Max was ordered to the pit for new, slick tires better suited to the unpredictable storm. Over the next few laps, the sandstorm cleared, and the asphalt quickly became damp. Team Red Bull's strategy paid off. Max's new slick tires stuck to the track like glue.

Lewis's tires didn't work as well with the changing conditions. By the last lap, the gap between Verstappen and Hamilton widened, clearing the way for Max to take the checkered flag.

Team Red Bull embraced the storm, demonstrating organizational agility. In a post-race debrief, Team Mercedes engineers bemoaned their caution and rigid adherence to the playbook. Mercedes chief strategist said, "We were too slow to adapt...We forgot that in F1, sometimes the best plans are the ones you throw away when the world starts spinning."

In fact, the world is always spinning! Organizational agility is a strategic approach to navigating perpetual motion in the world of business. Whether conditions move slowly or suddenly, they are always in motion. Change leadership requires organizational agility.

McKinsey[7] described the agile organization as one which "demonstrates the ability to quickly reconfigure strategy, structure, processes, people, and technology toward value-creating and value-protecting opportunities."

Agile organizations are both stable and dynamic at the same time.

Consider companies like Amazon, Meta, Alphabet (Google), or JP Morgan Chase. In the words of hockey great Wayne Gretzky, they skate to where the puck (or the business) is going. Agility enables change leadership. It provides a foundation for leaders to build on in developing the next chapter in an organization's story.

Developing your organization's agility requires leaders to:

Understand the characteristics of agility. By intentionally attuning attention to continually evolving conditions, then asking, "What does this motion mean to our customers, our customer engagement approach, our team members, our partners and suppliers," leaders elevate strategic awareness and enable adaptability. Understanding positions the company to "reconfigure strategy, structure, processes, people, and technology toward value-creating and value-protecting opportunities."

---

[7] How to create an agile organization, by Olli Salo, October 2, 2017, https://www.mckinsey.com/capabilities/people-and-organizational-performance/our-insights/how-to-create-an-agile-organization

Draw a distinction between "agility" and "change management." Agility is a skill that can be developed. It is the ability to make quick and effective adaptations to rapid condition changes. Agile individuals and organizations try new approaches, learn from mistakes, and embrace change. Change management is an event, project, or initiative. When the endeavor is complete, the organization moves on (or falls back to legacy habits).

Recognize that agility is an individual *and* organizational competency. Organizations are collections of individuals. Leaders must address the needs and concerns of both in elevating organizational agility. Identify team members who can easily translate subtle, gradual, rapid, or event-driven shifts in the external operating environment into implications for the business. By engaging individuals as agility advocates, collective agility rises.

Recognize the benefits of agility. Agility is a skill-based competency. Some team members have a natural agility proclivity, others may not. The benefit of organizational agility comes from *navigating* ongoing change vs. *confronting* it. When organizations attune to the perpetual motion of business operating conditions, agility becomes a navigation strategy.

Practice the Observer View. Ask: From a third-party view, what areas of my organization appear to be rigid, inflexible, or stuck? If I were a neutral third-party observer, what would catch my attention as a cue to demonstrate agility? What are some of the skills or knowledge areas where my organization needs an upgrade? What are my competitors doing that demonstrates agility?

Co-own identification of cues and clues prompting preemptive change with team members. Every team member can serve as an agility advocate. When leaders invite employees to identify and help address shifts in the way the company does business, they create engagement and elevate organizational agility. This includes viewing collection and interpreting environmental change indicators and opportunities for pre-emptive change business-as-usual activities.

Communicate agility as a core value. Telling the agility story is an ongoing endeavor. People need to see leaders communicate through demonstration and consistent verbalization of agility as an organizational value.

Where is your business today?

Here is a list of questions you and your team can use to foster conversation about your business's current level of agility, and inform next steps to raise organizational agility:

- How do we rate (high, medium, low) our company's level of agility today? In other words, how quickly do we reconfigure strategy, structure, processes, people and technology toward value-creating and value-protecting opportunities as conditions in our operating environment change?
- Which companies in our industry (or outside) demonstrate a high level of agility?
- What differences do we see between our company and the most agile companies?
- How does our company's current level of agility impact our customer experience?
- How does our company's current level of agility impact our employee experience?
- What risks are associated with our company's current level of agility?
- What would need to change at our company to rate your agility higher?

The story of dry farming wine grapes starts with business operating conditions. Dry farming is the art of growing grapes without supplemental irrigation. This approach is common in parts of the Mediterranean, South America, and California. In most cases, the dry farming business model is chosen based on operating conditions, in this case, lack of water access.

In California, drought conditions are common, making dry farming a viable option. Since the 1840s, when rainfall recording began in the state, California has been through a dozen extended droughts, the longest from 1928 to 1937 during the historical Dust Bowl period in the United States.

Paso Robles is a rapidly growing wine producing region in Central California. Subject to cyclical drought, its eleven viticultural areas offer winemakers topographical, soil, and rainfall diversity. Many of the region's award-winning vintners practice dry farming due to lack of water and because certain grape varieties are better suited for this approach.

Dry farming forces grapevine roots to dig deeper into the ground in search of water and nutrients. This stress strengthens the vine's connection to the soil and enables it to develop an extensive root system that can reach water sources hidden deep underground. Vines become stronger, more adaptable to changing conditions, and better able to self-regulate, especially in times of stress (changing, dry conditions); one might even say the vines become more agile! As a result, these agile vines produce grapes that are brighter and richer with deeper, more concentrated flavors. Dry-farmed grapes also develop thicker skins, which act as a natural barrier against pests and diseases.

Navigating change can feel like dry farming. Changing conditions, lack of certain resources, and discomfort with change can shake us at our roots. But when we recognize change for what it is (aka: business as usual), questions shift from "What happens *when* things change?" to "How do we navigate a perpetually changing operating environment?" This kind of shift is a step toward organizational agility.

Chapter 7
Which Niche? Get Clear About how you Want to Play

It's said that in Hollywood, there are only a handful of basic movie plots: David and Goliath, rags to riches, quest, comedy, tragedy, rebirth. Characters, twists and turns, and the details vary, but every movie storyline is built from these basics. In the business world, we can say the same thing. The basic competitive strategy plotlines are low-price leadership, product innovation, differentiation, or niche player.

As with movie storylines, a company chooses its fundamental operating strategy, then builds its business around the positioning. As examples, consider:

Walmart: Low-price leadership

Apple: Product innovation

Chipotle: Differentiation

Boeing Employees Credit Union: Niche player

In his seminal book *Competitive Strategy: Techniques for Analyzing Industries and Competitors*,[8] L. Michael Porter describes these foundational strategies in the context of an industry's competitive intensity. defined as the relative power of suppliers, level of threat from potential new industry participants, relative power of customers, level of threat from potential substitutes for

---

[8] https://www.amazon.com/Competitive-Strategy-Techniques-Industries-Competitors/dp/0684841487

the product or service, and the degree of competition among current industry participants.

With each strategy choice comes a set of supporting actions. A business competing as a low-price leader, for example, must apply its attention, resources, and objectives to driving costs as low as possible to succeed.

Product innovators, meanwhile, disproportionately invest in research and development to populate a pipeline of new, monetizable ideas.

Differentiators focus on what makes their offering unique and of value to customers.

And, finally, niche players build and sustain competency, and earn relevance with their specific, unique clientele.

A frequent challenge arises when a business either loses clarity about its competitive positioning or drifts from its strengths.

In December 2020, JCPenney emerged from Chapter 11 bankruptcy. When the company filed for bankruptcy in March of that year, CNN reported, "The pandemic was the final blow to a 118-year-old company struggling to overcome a decade of bad decisions, executive instability and damaging marketing trends."

The retailer was founded by James Cash Penney in 1902 as the Golden Rule dry goods store in Kemmerer, Wyoming. Penney's business philosophy was simple: Treat others as we would like to be treated. This approach worked well, fueling the company's rapid growth. In 1913, the company incorporated as the J. C. Penney Stores Company, with 34 stores in the Western United States. In 1927, J.C. Penney Co. went public, with its stock trading on the NYSE. By 1929, the company operated 1,392 retail stores offering reasonably priced products in rural communities.

JCPenney's success in part was due to knowing who their customers were and what they valued. The company built its' brand serving budget-conscious families. Over time they offered affordable mid-range clothing, beauty products and household goods for their target customers. The business operating model was so successful, it inspired a young employee, Sam Walton, who began a job at JCPenney in 1940, to venture off and start his own retailing business, Walmart, in 1962.

Like all organizations, JCPenney operates in a business environment characterized by perpetual motion. Over time, company leaders adapted better to some changes than others. In the early 1960s customers and their expectations changed. So did the competitive landscape for retailers with a shift to discount stores as Walmart entered the market. To address these shifts, in 1962 JCPenney entered the discount merchandising market segment through acquisition of General Merchandise Company, which operated a low-price retailer known as The Treasury stores. The strategy proved unsuccessful and was discontinued in 1981. On the other hand, JCPenney was an early ecommerce adopter, offering items for sale online in 1994, the year Amazon was founded.

In 2010, a significant strategic misstep unfolded as JCPenney lost sight of its core customer base. Revenue was on the decline, and the company decided to attempt a high-end fashion makeover, partnering with celebrity designers, and introducing boutiques within stores. The plan to move up-market required a major investment, but alienated JCPenney's core customer base (budget-conscious families) and confused the high-end market.

The result of this strategy shift was a decline in sales, layoffs, and store closures. The company eventually returned to its core value proposition with some success, but the detour inflicted lasting damage. While not the only factor in the company's 2020 bankruptcy, stepping outside of its' target market was a contributing element.

It is too soon to know whether JCPenney's refocus on offering affordable merchandise to the company's core clientele will succeed in the long-term, but there are signs of progress. In late 2023, CNBC reported[9] that JCPenney, "Plans to invest more than $1 billion by the end of 2025 in a bid to revive the storied but troubled 121-year-old department store chain. The money will go toward remodeling JCPenney stores, upgrading its online shopping site and app, and making its supply network more efficient so that online orders are delivered more quickly." CEO Marc Rosen, who took the helm in November 2021, said, "These changes have helped increase the number of repeat visits of existing customers to stores and online. More than 50 million customers have visited JCPenney in the past three years."

For JCPenney and every business, it is essential to know who your customers are, what they value, how to serve them, and to create the most impactful business model in context of a dynamic operating environment. For example, community banks are either niche players or differentiators, not low-cost providers. Their customers tend to value personal relationships with a bank over higher deposit rates or lower loan rates. Occasionally, a community bank will deploy a strategy to pay high deposit rates to attract new deposit customers. The result: Transitory deposits from non-customers always looking for the next best deal.

---

[9] https://www.cnbc.com/2023/08/31/jcpenney-is-spending-1-billion-on-store-and-online-upgrades-in-latest-bid-to-revive-its-business.html#:~:text=Under%20new%20owners%20%E2%80%94%20mall%20companies,its%20bankruptcy%20filing%2C%20Rosen%20said.

Another common strategy misalignment appears when high-volume manufacturers get the itch to niche (think General Motors developing the Saturn brand or United Airlines with their Ted brand). The most common result: suboptimal outcomes. Large, high-volume businesses tend to overengineer their niche experiments, add excessive structure and administration to the venture, and create an economic burden that defeats the purpose of a niche play.

How to Define Your Competitive Strategy

Defining, designing, and deploying competitive strategy is like playing chess. It requires future thinking while leading from now. Analyzing the chess board involves considering potential consequences of each move, assessing risks and rewards, and determining the best course of action. The chess player considers their opponent's range of possible moves, strengths, and weaknesses, then plans responses several steps in advance. Successful chess players demonstrate agility, adapting strategies mid-game to respond to unexpected moves or unforeseen circumstances. Winning a chess game isn't just about making the best next move; it's about achieving a long-term objective. Both chess and business have finite resources - pieces in chess and capital (human, intellectual, physical, financial) in business. Making the most of these resources involves careful allocation and prioritization, focusing on high-impact activities that optimize return on investment.

As you consider set-up of your company's chessboard, these actionable ideas will help affirm a competitive strategy that fits your business characteristics and competencies:

Get clear about your company's competencies and capacity. Defining the best positioning for a company's competitive strategy requires candid assessment of available resources and scale, which combined represent capacity. Is your company's capacity aligned with low-volume production, high-volume, high value-add, or limited value-add? What are the organization's core competencies and how do they align with capacity? How will the company build its competencies? How do your firm's competencies compare with those of your competitors, and how does this inform competitive positioning? Organizational competencies (like capturing continuous efficiency gains, innovativeness, distinctive customer engagement approach, natural niches) are opportunities to build upon and add color to your business's competitive positioning. These questions help determine how you solidify your competitive position.

Be clear about who you serve. In chapter 4 we discussed risks emanating from lack of a clearly defined target customer or specific segments. The principle – knowing who your customer is, what they value, and what they'll pay for - applies to the development of competitive strategy. When answers to these questions are not clearly defined, the business model is weakened and opportunities for competitors open. Conversely, addressing specific customers with specific needs strengthens a company's competitive positioning. Gluten Free Foods Company is unequivocally clear in the target market they serve: Consumers who eat gluten free pasta. That's it! When JCPenney added high-end fashion brands to their offering, their target customer became unclear.

Get clear about how you want to play the game. Understand your target customers, your company's competencies and capacity, and the best way to compete. Is the company structured to be a low-price leader, or better aligned with differentiation? Is the firm a product innovator, always offering something new and engaging, or is a better way to focus on a unique set of customer needs? Candidly answering these questions helps set up the chess board for an engaging game.

The National Weather Service describes the Fujiwhara effect as an intense dance around the common center of two different hurricanes. The storms spin each other around for a while before moving off on their own paths, or they gravitate towards each other until they reach a common point and merge (aka: hurricane collision). Lacking a clearly defined competitive strategy can lead a business into Fujiwhara-type conditions.

With an objective view into your company's best competitive strategy positioning, it is easy to identify activities that do not align. If the business has drifted into a danger zone (for instance, you find that new customers are only interested in low prices, but your operating costs don't support heavy discounts), it's time to do a competitive strategy alignment assessment. You may find activities that should be discontinued or refined to align with your foundational competitive strategy.

Chapter 8
Preventing Strategy Scope Creep

My daughter encountered scope creep recently after spotting a cockroach in her Queens, N.Y., apartment building. In a moment of courage (for someone with insect phobia), she grabbed a broom and a dustpan, scooped up the cockroach, and quickly walked the insect out the front door to dispose of it outside. She felt a great sense of accomplishment with the successful completion of this feat.

Unfortunately, standing in her pajamas at 2:30 a.m. in front of her apartment, with no door key or cell phone, she realized the building's self-locking door had closed tight after she stepped outside. A project with a simple, singular purpose — disposing of an annoying cockroach — had now expanded to something much larger.

Scope creep is common in the business world. An organization without a clearly defined business vision gets so far away from its' original reason for existing, it becomes unrecognizable. The consequences of scope creep include strategic distractions, business model suboptimization, inefficiency, financial disruptions, morale damage, and overall poor performance.

Are you causing scope creep?

Scope creep is usually unintentional. Leaders undertake a single action that deviates from the company's definition of success, and all appears to be well. Then comes the next step outside the vision, then a third. Initially, leaders convince themselves of their decision-making acumen until results disprove this perception.

Perhaps *un*conventional wisdom — the perception that because we think differently in our organization, we must be right – plays a role in strategy scope creep. When leaders hold this mindset, they expose their organizations to the risk of taking on activities that may not be a good fit. This is not to say a company should never expand its activities; it means leaders need to dig deeper to understand an activity pattern that will contribute to (or distract from) organizational success.

Other contributors to strategy scope creep include:

Unclear vision. Vision is how the organization defines success. Vision informs priorities, which distill into strategies, then operating activities. If vision is not clearly defined, frequently communicated, or well understood, strategy scope creep can easily unfold.

Poorly defined priorities. Vision informs a short list (three-to-five is ideal) of organizational operating priorities. Poorly defined priorities create confusion. "Our top priority is growth" is meaningless. Here's an example of clear priorities for a business insurance company: underwriting effectiveness, loss prevention, net-new client growth (comprised of new client acquisition and existing client retention), and talent development. These four priorities support the company's vision: "We serve as our clients' trusted risk management advisor and insurer for the life of their business." With this clarity, team members and leaders know the most meaningful areas of attention and resource allocation for the company; equally important, these priorities communicate what is out of scope for the company. Activities outside these priorities should be avoided. Priorities can evolve or come to completion over time, and when that happens, capacity frees up to consider new priorities.

Too many priorities. *Good to Great* author Jim Collins wrote, "If you have more than three priorities, you don't have any." The soundness of Collins' strict view emphasizes this principle: A long list of priorities dilutes effectiveness and creates distraction.

Poor communication or absence of communication when strategy scope creeps. Leaders need to hold themselves, their peers and team members accountable to stay in strategy scope. Calling out exceptions is proper governance to prevent scope creep.

Changes in the leadership team. New leaders may (and should) assess the company's vision and priorities to determine relevance; this is prudent strategic leadership. Once they reaffirm the company's vision and priorities, the focus shifts to prudent governance.

In 2002, Nick Woodman embarked on a five-month surfing tour to Australia and Indonesia. Five years earlier, Nick graduated with a degree in visual arts from the University of California, San Diego, where he enhanced his skills as an amateur photographer. As a surfer, Nick wanted to shoot pictures while riding waves, but photography technology of the time was not designed to meet his interests or budget. Nick's interest and creativity spurred the creation of an action camera called GoPro. The camera gave birth to a company focused on the connected sports genre.

Over the next decade, GoPro rode a wave of success. Its' reasonably priced, durable, user-friendly cameras were a hit with extreme sports enthusiasts, adventurous travelers, and social media influencers. However, a case of strategy scope creep eventually threatened to destabilize the company's success.

GoPro went public in 2014. As a public company, their investors held high expectations for GoPro's growth, creating pressure on Nick and his team to expand its market share and profits. GoPro leadership elected to become a mainstream consumer electronics company. They took on bold, exciting projects like developing drones, 360-degree view cameras, and virtual reality platforms. Each new endeavor was intended to diversify GoPro's offerings and open doors to new customer segments.

Enthusiasm for GoPro's expanding menu of offerings didn't last long. The drone market was oversaturated and intensely competitive by the time GoPro entered. The 360-degree camera offering missed the mark in terms of functionality. The VR platform was introduced with great fanfare but never gained traction over established competitors.

As new endeavors captured management's time and attention, GoPro's core customers began to feel neglected. Product releases slowed. Camera features became stale. Customer loyalty began to decline. Strategy scope creep caused the company to bleed cash and build frustration. To survive, in late 2016, and again in early 2017, GoPro laid off employees - more than 500 people (25% of the company's workforce). Fox Business named Nick one of the worst CEOs of the year. Without re-grounding, the GoPro story might have ended here.

By 2016, GoPro's adventure into consumer electronics had become a costly distraction away from the foundation of their success. Fortunately, Nick and company leaders recognized the root causes and took ownership of leading change. GoPro refocused on their core business - action cameras. They invested in new features, better software, and targeted marketing campaigns. The company streamlined operations, discontinued unprofitable ventures and pared-back their product line.

In an interview with *The Gate* in early 2020, Nick said his company was going to "Focus on serving users and developing software that suits them." He said, "Whatever GoPro produces *this year and next*, consumers can surely count on a *return to the authenticity, simplicity*, and *eye-catching adventure* products that built the brand's enormous success in the first place."

Getting back on track took time. Eventually, GoPro reconnected with its core customer base and reestablished brand loyalty. Today, the company is stable with a clear focus on who their customers are, and what matters most to them. Their mission - sharing experiences around the world – guides the business in all its activities.

The GoPro story is a real-life example of an organization pulled into strategy scope creep. It's a reminder that while diversification can be a path to growth, it must be embarked on intentionally and strategically. The focus must be on priorities aligned with a vision.

What to ask before embarking on something new

In the GoPro case, scope creep led the company away from what it did extremely well. The questions they *didn't* ask before expanding activities were: Who are our customers? What do our customers expect? What are our company's core competencies? How do those competencies apply in each of our markets? Who are our competitors, and how will we compete in new product areas?

Scope creep is avoidable when leaders ask:

- How does this new (or expanded) activity align with our definition of success or our company's vision?
- How do our core competencies lend themselves to this activity/strategy?
- How would engaging in this activity/strategy impact our human and capital resources?
- How would we ensure that engaging in this new activity/strategy will not distract from our primary business objectives?
- What conditions lead us to believe this is the right time to engage in this new activity/strategy?

Taking a deep dive into these questions can help leaders make a distinction between strategy scope creep and the need for business model refinement.

Back in Queens, my daughter worked through the best available options to get back inside her apartment that night, (after disposing of the offending cockroach) with no luck. She spent hours trying to wake up local family, friends, and neighbors to ask for help, all to no avail. She ended up sitting in a corner of a 24-hour CVS until daylight when a neighbor was available to unlock the door and let her into the building.

She will always remember this scope creep moment. I suspect she will flush the next cockroach.

Chapter 9
How People Development Makes a Company More Competitive

Long ago, in a bustling valley nestled between towering mountains stood the renowned Sunstone Foundry. For generations, it crafted exquisite objects that shimmered with magic, drawing merchants from across the land. Yet, a shadow gnawed at the heart of the foundry. Profits dwindled and whispers of decline echoed through its dusty halls.

Meister Ashcroft, Sunstone's leader, became distressed. He scoured ancient texts seeking forgotten formulas and lost enchantments to address the foundry's issues. He hired renowned advisors and lured skilled artisans from distant lands to help change Sunstone's path. Still, the Sunstone Foundry floundered, its once radiant glow dimming.

One moonlit night, Ashcroft leaned against a cold furnace, despair gnawing at him. A flicker of movement caught his eye - a young apprentice, Elara, meticulously arranging scraps of discarded metal on the workshop floor. Intrigued, Ashcroft watched as she hammered and twisted the shards, her brow furrowed in concentration.

Slowly, under Elara's nimble fingers, the scraps emerged into a delicate form. Light danced within the metal. Not the vibrant fire Ashcroft sought, but a soft, luminescent glow that warmed the room. This, Elara explained, was not a weapon or jewel, but a lantern, meant to cast light in the darkest corners.

Ashcroft scoffed. "This paltry trinket will not save our foundry."

Elara looked him in the eye. "Meister Ashcroft, perhaps our greatest treasures are not hidden in forgotten texts or distant lands," she said with gentle words. "Perhaps they lie right here, in the hands of those who dare to imagine, to create, to find beauty in the discarded."

Her words sparked a flicker of hope within Ashcroft. He began to see the foundry anew, not as a fading relic, but as a wellspring of creativity. He empowered Elara and her fellow apprentices, and encouraged them to experiment, to challenge tradition, to find magic in the everyday.

Slowly, the foundry transformed. Walls once hung with cobwebs were adorned with sketches and prototypes. Laughter and hammering echoed through the halls. The discarded scraps took shape as wondrous inventions: wind chimes that whispered stories, lamps that flickered with firefly light, locks that opened with laughter.

The Sunstone Foundry once again became a beacon of innovation. Merchants flocked to Sunstone for the simple magic that warmed their hearts and lit their paths. It wasn't the forgotten enchantments or imported skills that saved the foundry, but the spark of creativity rekindled within its own walls.

Meister Ashcroft gazed at the bustling foundry bathed in the gentle glow of Elara's lantern and finally understood. The greatest treasures of the Sunstone Foundry weren't found in distant lands, but in the hearts and minds of its own people. They were the treasures of imagination, of collaboration, of finding beauty in the seemingly ordinary. And these, he realized, were the most valuable treasures of all.

Every year, businesses spend billions of dollars to look outside their company to find new ideas, answers, and opportunities to build competitive advantages, while overlooking their greatest resource – their team members. As in the Sunstone Foundry parable, engaged employees can be a company's most valuable treasures.

Organization leaders hear it every day: "It's difficult finding qualified employees." "People don't want to return to in-person work." "Now we have to think about employee well-being; what's next!"

The premise of this book is business operating conditions are in perpetual motion. Evidence demonstrates customers change, competition changes, how businesses engage with customers changes, technology supporting the business changes, and the economics of the business changes. Under this thesis, it follows that employees change. Who they are, what they value, what they expect from your firm, and your firm's value proposition to employees are different now than five years ago, and than they will be five years hence.

Leading from Now in the human capital arena requires attunement to the dynamic nature of people. Research tells us that intentional actions by management to spark employee engagement yield disproportionate results. Gallup's State of the Global Workplace 2023 Report, The Voice of the World's Employees, estimates, "Low [employee] engagement costs the global economy $8.8 trillion. That's 9% of global GDP — enough to make the difference between success and failure for humanity."

Gallup's report states, "Poor management leads to lost customers and lost profits and leads to miserable lives. Gallup's research into wellbeing at work finds that having a job you hate is worse than being unemployed, and those negative emotions end up at home, impacting relationships with family. If you're not thriving at work, you're unlikely to thrive at life."

Overlooking these findings and the essential responsibility of leaders to engage and develop people is tantamount to organizational failure. Navigating change is a team sport; disengagement of team members has a deleterious effect on outcomes.

Contemplate the business operating environment your team members experience. In addition to continually changing conditions, studies tell us workers' stress and anxiety levels have not subsided post-pandemic. Certainly, building organizational agility (detailed in Chapter 6) is an important ingredient in people development, but there is more.

What does it mean to create an engaging environment for your team? According to Gallup, employee engagement reflects the "involvement and enthusiasm of employees in their work and workplace. Employees can become engaged when their basic needs are met and when they have a chance to contribute, a sense of belonging, and opportunities to learn and grow."

Engaged employees thrive at work. "They are highly involved in and enthusiastic about their work and workplace. They are psychological *owners*, drive performance and innovation, and move the organization forward. In contrast, disengaged employees are psychologically unattached to their work and company. Because their engagement needs are not being fully met, they're putting time but not energy or passion into their work. Actively disengaged employees aren't just unhappy at work. They resent that their needs aren't being met and act out their unhappiness. Every day, these workers potentially undermine what their engaged coworkers accomplish."

Gallup determines employee engagement levels through uncovering agreement with statements like, "I know what is expected of me at work." "I have the opportunity to do what I do best every day." "My supervisor, or someone at work, seems to care about me as a person." "There is someone at work who encourages my development." and "At work, my opinions seem to count."

In business, competition for the highest value resources — human, physical, economic, noneconomic — is constant. Demand ebbs and flows, but each organization is in competition for resources that advance its' vision of success.

Today's competition for human resources has taken on new dimensions. In the past, conventional wisdom said offering competitive compensation and benefits was all an organization needed to do. Today, that is just the ante to be in the game. Differentiating an organization through people development enhances its ability to attract the best available employees and demonstrates a core commitment to successfully navigate change.

Why Differentiate with People Development?

Strategy thought leader Michael Porter defines differentiation as making your products or services different from, and more attractive than, those of your competitors. In the context of a competitive go-to-market strategy, a business's choices are clear: Operate as either a low-cost leader, innovator, differentiator, or niche player. *Leading from Now* includes application of this concept to people development strategy.

Here are five ideas to differentiate your business as a people developer:

Redefine management position descriptions. Every management role is a people development position, and job descriptions need to reflect this responsibility. This means holding all managers accountable for investing in talent development. Gallup provides outcomes for effective people development and team engagement. For instance, clear, consistent communications, understanding each team member and their aspirations, and regular performance conversation (not only a year-end performance review) leads employees to affirm, "I know what is expected of me at work." "I have the opportunity to do what I do best every day." "My supervisor, or someone at work, seems to care about me as a person." "There is someone at work who encourages my development." and "At work, my opinions seem to count."

New employee onboarding. First impressions last. Making onboarding an extraordinary experience sets the tone. Onboarding is much more than completing documents and delivering the employee handbook. Employers can help new team members avoid potential cognitive dissonance about their new job through a clearly defined Day One, Week One, Month One road map that includes ample connections with colleagues, exposure to company culture, and frequent check-ins on matriculation through the onboarding experience.

Purpose-driven mentoring. With a clear purpose centered in individual development, mentoring can be impactful. Well-designed mentoring programs include the intentional pairing of mentor and mentee, regular engagement, defined activities, and goals. Clarity about what mentoring is not (i.e., coaching, sponsoring or a guaranteed path to promotion) helps align expectations.

Career pathing. A recent Society for Human Resource Management study showed more than half of workers said they need to learn new skills.[10]

within the next year to continue their careers, and 46% said they are not as skilled as they need to be. When it comes to delivering structure around individual development, few organizations stand out. The opportunity: Create a strategy for formal individual development plans, co-owned by employees and their managers. Review plans at least semi-annually and update accordingly.

Career deceleration. Workforce composition is changing, getting younger and older at the same time. Much emphasis is placed on accelerating Generation Z members in their careers, while at the other end of the range, many younger baby boomers and older Gen-Xers are interested in changing the pace or calibration of their work. A mindful approach to capitalizing on team members' ability to contribute in a different way than people who are earlier in their career creates talent-sharing opportunities that often are overlooked.

Many organizations miss the opportunity to differentiate themselves as people development exemplars, and instead, unintentionally, become talent consumers. Operating as a talent

---

[10] (**Employees Want Additional Opportunities for Career, Skills Development,** March 24, 2022, byPaul Bergeron - https://www.shrm.org/topics-tools/news/organizational-employee-development/employees-want-additional-opportunities-career-skills-development#: text =Workers%20need%20more%20skills%20development,of%20employers%20believe %20the%20same).

consumer can relegate the firm to competing for human resources based on compensation alone.

Organizations can make intentional decisions about their people development philosophy. Differentiation as a people development exemplar requires a well-thought-out competitive strategy, implemented through engaged managers who understand the value of the human capital they steward. Sound bites like "people matter most here" or "people are our competitive advantage" are hollow unless supported by strategy and actions aligned with nurturing and development of highly valued human resources.

Chapter 10
Navigating the Leadership Rip Currents of Change

While navigating a rough, foggy ocean, a battleship's radar suddenly indicates an object directly in its path. The ship's captain sends a radio signal saying, "We are on a collision course. I advise you to change course 10 degrees north immediately."

A response crackles over the radio: "Negative. We advise you to change course 10 degrees south."

The captain can now see a blinking light from the approaching object. Frustrated, he replies: "I'm this ship's captain. I command you to change course 10 degrees north immediately!"

"I'm a controller, second class," came a reply. "Advise that you change course 10 degrees south to avoid imminent collision."

At this point, the furious captain yells: "This is a battleship! Change *your* course immediately!"

After briefly pausing, the captain hears a calm reply: "This is a lighthouse. Your call on what you want to do."

Navigating changing conditions can be a challenge, even for the most skilled leaders. This chapter discusses actionable ideas to elevate leaders' acumen in navigating change.

Conditions: The invitation to change.

One definition of the word "condition" is a particular state of being of a person or thing with respect to circumstances. This definition excludes the fact that most conditions are subject to change. And while the velocity of change varies from condition to condition, rarely are changes permanent.

Continually changing business operating conditions are expected. What is new is the rate, breadth, and depth of change for businesses. Consider the public text-sharing app space. X, formerly Twitter, took five years to reach 100 million users; Meta Threads took five days to achieve the same number of users. Overnight disruption to the 10th degree! Imagine the dynamic in the competitive landscape: advertisers contemplating where and how to reallocate their spending or businesses reconsidering implications for public text-sharing as part of the social media strategy.

Time will tell the value of either text-sharing platform. Yet, this illustration of change velocity provides a clear message: *Operating conditions can change quickly and substantively in anticipated and unexpected ways.*

Following the 9/11 terrorist attacks, the United States Army War College began using the acronym VUCA to describe a substantively different and unfamiliar international security environment: volatile (unpredictable, rapid change), uncertain (current environment is unclear, future is uncertain), complex (plethora of interconnected elements come into play with the potential to create chaos and confusion) and ambiguous (lack of clarity or awareness about situations). VUCA characteristics apply to business operating conditions and those affecting international security.

In navigating change, evolving conditions are an invitation to adjust. Questions for leaders become: How and when do we address this invitation for change? Part of the answer lies in the evolving condition itself. What are the first indicators that a business condition (or conditions) is changing? Are these conditions changing slowly or rapidly? What are the benefits and risks of adjusting now vs. further into changing conditions? What is the case for change that will engage our stakeholders? How will we communicate evolving conditions and the case for change to our stakeholders?

Rip Currents: The Force of Resistance

Recently at Newport Beach, every lifeguard station on the Balboa Peninsula had red rip current flags raised. El Niño weather conditions created outsized waves and a strong undercurrent. Rip currents are powerful currents of water flowing away from shore. They can pull swimmers and surfers away from the shore, past the line of breaking waves. These undercurrents are very powerful and dangerous.

In navigating change, human undercurrents present a significant risk. Like rip currents at the beach, these undercurrents resist change, pulling people back to their perceived status quo. Change resistance can show up as discomfort, fear, misinformation, distrust, or unwillingness to adjust to new conditions. In opposition to VUCA conditions, most people look for consistent patterns and predictability. Resistance may have been on Woodrow Wilson's mind when he said, "If you want to make enemies, try to change something."

Resistance to change can be a debilitating obstacle to an organization's progress and adaptability to dynamic operating conditions. Yogi Berra said, "Baseball is 90% mental. The other half is physical." Keeping math accuracy in mind, it is fair to say that navigating change is 90% mental and 10% everything else. Change efforts fail more often than they succeed because leaders frequently fall short of making a compelling case for change, overlook employees' perceptions about the change experience, and fail to communicate with team members effectively and consistently.

In navigating forces of resistance to change, leaders can elevate their probability of success by addressing these questions: How will we communicate our case for change? How will we create a sense of co-ownership in our change initiatives? In what ways can we ensure effective, ongoing two-way communications with all stakeholders as we navigate our change initiatives? How will we gain and sustain insights into team members' perspectives about our change initiatives? When inevitable challenges arise in our change initiatives, how will we engage team members in adjusting and adapting our plans?

Why is Change such a Challenge?

Confucius said, "Life is quite simple, but we insist on making it complicated." The most crucial factor in successfully navigating change is earning and sustaining the buy-in of the people executing the changes. So simple, so complicated. The complication comes from overlooking the essentiality of earning and maintaining buy-in.

In *Leading from Zero: Seven Essential Elements of Earning Relevance*,[11] I distill the need into *winning the hearts and minds* of stakeholders (employees in particular). Bain & Co. studied the question: Why is it so difficult to make change take root? The company's *Results Delivery: Busting Three Common Myths of Change Management* report[12] looks at barriers to successful change management at 184 global companies. The company found that

---

[11] https://www.amazon.com/Leading-Zero-Essential-Elements-Relevance/dp/1734409916
[12] https://www.bain.com/insights/results-delivery-busting-3-common-change-management-myths/

65% of initiatives required "significant behavioral change on the part of employees — something managers often fail to consider and plan for in advance." In addition, 63% of companies analyzed faced "high risks to their change efforts because of significant communications gaps between the leaders of the effort and the employees most affected by it." Bain found many companies assume they can succeed with the right combination of strong incentives for their leaders. Yet, they overlook the importance of building employee commitment during a change effort.

Leaders must win team members' hearts and minds to effectively navigate change by creating a pull toward the precise definition of success (the vision). Leaders must create an environment that empowers people to make an impact through their ideas and actions, aligned with the organization's vision. This happens by actively defining, designing, and delivering a culture where team members co-own the organization's path through changes. Leaders own setting the tone for active engagement, collaboration, and nurturing esprit de corps. A deep level of co-ownership and shared dominion over the organization's future state can emerge by creating emotional engagement with the team, aligned with the business's goals in navigating changes.

Navigating Change

Effective change leadership is not an event. It is a proactive, ongoing process that requires an organization to sustain a laser focus on continually evolving conditions within their business and across their external operating environment. Change leadership is an opportunity to create co-ownership in navigating the continually evolving business operating environment.

Recognizing and addressing the invitation to change, identifying and overcoming resistance forces, and understanding the keys to uncomplicating the process are core to navigating change, creating and sustaining buy-in across stakeholders, inspiring participation in the transformation at hand, and maintaining focus.

Chapter 11
Taking the Helm as Navigator

Leading from Now: A Leader's Guide to Navigating Change. I chose this title intentionally. The notion of *navigating* change resonates with me. One definition of the term navigation is: *the art and science of determining the position of a ship, plane, or other vehicle, and guiding it to a specific destination; navigation requires a person to know the vehicle's current location and travel conditions enroute to the desired destination.* A perfect metaphor for leaders operating in an environment of perpetual motion is: A clearly defined destination pulled into decisions made *now*. This is the leader's role.

As a strategy consultant, most of my work involves guiding businesses in navigating change, so I feel comfortable with these principles. I've also had the opportunity to experience performing the change leader role operating businesses for others and practice the principles of *Leading from Now*.

Over the past five years, I've served as an interim CEO on four different occasions. In each case, the departure of the previous CEO came about sooner than the organization's board of directors expected. With each business I saw a need to embrace a change leadership approach. These experiences put me in situations where I needed to ask and answer the question: since navigating change is business as usual, how do I need to refine my approach to leadership?

As I've contemplated this question over time, I've had to challenge my beliefs about myself, people I work with, organizations, and business overall. Specific to navigating change, I've uncovered two contradictory beliefs I need to manage.

First, there are times that I feel when it comes to operating the business and addressing changing conditions, *most people* I work with have views like mine. Second, there are times my feeling is *nobody* holds views about the business like mine. Both perspectives can be unfounded and have also led me to confirmation bias (the tendency to favor information that confirms or strengthens a belief). Both beliefs have been barriers to my effectiveness in leading change.

Awareness of these challenges has been an important step in elevating my change leadership acumen. Serving as an interim CEO also produced an actionable set of learnings directly related to navigating organizational change for any leader, family business founder, team leader, division head or CEO.

Seek Ongoing Stakeholder Engagement

Key stakeholders include customers (beneficiaries in the nonprofit arena), team members, investors, vendors, regulators, and in some cases, community leaders. Whether changing business operating conditions are taking place within or outside an organization, understanding stakeholders, their priorities, expectations, and concerns plays a role critical role in navigating change.

In times of anticipated changes (key employee departures, operating missteps, or public relations issues), proactive stakeholder engagement shifts from important to important and urgent. Outreach, sharing authentic messages, inviting input, and sharing concerns and ideas elevate stakeholder engagement; minimizing or ignoring the importance of these relationships is deleterious.

I worked with a bank investment division to address an operating model issue. Prior to my involvement, regulators examining the division voiced their risk concerns to management. In conversation with a regulator examining the issue, the division CEO was overheard saying, "The way we operate our business is really none of your business, it's ours." The regulator, a relevant stakeholder in this business, was not impressed with the CEO's bravado. Two weeks after the interaction, the bank was notified of Matter Requiring Attention (MRA) from the regulator. The MRA included a description of substantive consequences for the bank in the event management didn't resolve its operating model issues forthwith. This case represents a missed opportunity and unpleasant consequences for key stakeholder engagement.

Uncertainty is Constant, Even when Conditions Appear Otherwise

Conditions under which I performed each interim CEO role were turbulent. In one case, a beloved CEO had the opportunity of a lifetime to lead another, larger organization. There was no clear internal successor, which created angst among some employees and company leaders. Uncertainty level: Moderate.

In another case, the previous CEO was only in the role for a short time when he realized his calling was elsewhere. He provided the board with a short transition period before moving to his new position. This was toward the end of Covid lockdowns, and the business was still dealing with the significant impact of the pandemic. Uncertainty level: High.

Two additional cases held similar circumstances. I entered the interim CEO position after each company's board decided to part ways with an existing CEO. There was no malfeasance, simply benign neglect each board elected to address. Employees, partners, and customers were surprised by what they perceived to be an unexpected, rapid change of leaders. Uncertainty level: Very High.

With each of these cases, I learned that even before the prior CEO's departure, the company had experienced uncertainty. From the outside (and to some on the inside), these companies appeared to be operating in a steady state. In reality, the only steady thing was the perpetual motion of operating conditions. Clear cues indicating it was time to refine the business operating model went unaddressed.

The learning: Change leadership means proactive, ongoing adaptation of an organization to its operating environment, which is in perpetual motion (also commonly defined as "uncertainty"). Leaders must be attuned to conditions in the present moment to infer and inform actions taken today, aligned with future state success. Business go-to-market operating models have a finite shelf-life, and require regular refreshment, refinement, or replacement. Leaders decide to intentionally initiate change or react to forces evolving the organization.

Be Clear about what I'm Here to Do

Each interim role started suddenly. Direction from the boards was clear but limited. None of the organizations had a concise business plan fitting current conditions I could pick up and execute. This ambiguity during times of uncertainty presented me with a simple question: What am I here to do?

It was clear that placing CEO decisions on hold pending a new, permanent top executive was not the right approach. Particularly in times of elevated uncertainty, stakeholders (employees, customers, owners) need clarity in the moment. Sometimes that means describing current operating environment conditions as a path to discussions about what to do now, or next.

Knowing what I am here to do exemplifies the practice of *Leading from Now*. And describing current operating environment conditions enabled me to shift from *What is* to *What if* scenario planning for each business. I learned *What if* conversations among team members helps uncover opportunities, concerns, and individual challenges with a company's current reality and future state path. The better change leaders understand where their teammates are in their organizational agility, the greater the impact they can have.

The learning: Leaders' understanding of what they are here to do extends beyond a job description. Engaging team members in current reality conversations (what is), shifting the dialog to future state success (what if), enables leaders to quickly get to root-cause issues and begin developing organizational agility.

There is a Way Forward and You Play a Role

A common question among employees is: Do I matter to this organization? Gallup Employee Engagement data suggests that most businesses don't do a great job of addressing this question.

As an interim CEO, I've heard this question many times. Elevated uncertainty becomes personal when companies go through sudden or unforeseen change. I've learned that an effective answer (assuming it is true) is this: There is a way forward for our organization, and you play a role in our journey. This statement opens the door to inquiry and inviting team member feedback: How do you see our path forward? What does success look like for our company in your view? What are the most important issues we need to address today? What role do you see yourself playing as we move forward?

This type of dialog creates openness, trust, and transparency.

Transparency doesn't mean saying everything; it means openness and candor for the betterment of the organization. I was on a flight from Phoenix to Tampa that was delayed at the gate for mechanical reasons. The pilot announced that our plane had a burnt-out wingtip light that needed to be replaced before the flight could be approved for takeoff. After 45 minutes, the pilot returned with another announcement. "There's some good news and bad news. The good news is we found another Airbus A321 wingtip light. The bad news: it's on another A321 in the service bay, so the mechanic needs to remove the lamp for that plane, then install it on ours." Complete transparency? Yes. But as a passenger, I didn't need to know the airline was Frankensteining one airplane by taking parts from another.

The learning: Team member engagement is the responsibility of leaders. It doesn't just happen. Engagement requires intention, attention, and discipline. Given the perpetual motion of business conditions, earning and sustaining team member engagement is an ongoing endeavor.

Hurry up and be Strategic

Strategic management is an ongoing leadership activity. Each company I served treated strategic *planning* as an event; develop the plan, check the box, then go about your business. When strategic management, which includes change leadership, is understood as an ongoing business as usual activity, leaders are positioned to ask: what activities should I engage in today to have the greatest impact on tomorrow's results?

There is value in deep-dive, formal strategic planning activities, but there is little evidence that investing 90 days in the process yields significantly better results than an accelerated effort. My interim CEO experience taught me that defining a definition of success (vision), and a short list of strategic priorities empowers a team to make meaningful progress in a short time.

The learning: The benefits of a strategic management approach (including change leadership) can accrue in short order. This doesn't exclude the value of a formal strategic planning process. Instead, it means the sooner a leader can affirm (or define) the organization's vision and top strategic priorities, the sooner they can make a meaningful impact.

Recognize the Difference Between Personal Dominion vs. Control

A natural reaction to navigating changing conditions is to want to take control. It comes from the need for security and order when we face the unknown, fear of vulnerability in challenging, and a cognitive bias known as the illusion of control – the natural tendency to believe we have more control over situations than we do.

Leaders are not exempt from attempting to control situations, particularly during times of rapid change. When a golfer squeezes their club grip too tightly, the ball usually ends up in a different place than intended. Outcomes for leaders taking a tight grip on the organization are similar; things do not advance as hoped.

I've learned this lesson many times. Jumping into an organization in motion as interim CEO elevated my perception that I should (could) take control to create stability. I found that a better approach is recognizing *influence* as the best tool in my toolkit. Inviting stakeholder engagement, soliciting team members' ideas about current reality and the path forward are meaningful strategies to create collaboration, reduce fear, and stimulate forward movement.

I also discovered the benefits of exercising personal dominion over my thoughts, actions, and countenance. Business is about people, and we are feeling, thinking, acting creatures (not always in this order).

Dominion means ownership. I own my mindset and how I show up in the business. If I have control over anything, this is it. I cannot control views, values, emotions, or actions of others, but I certainly have dominion over myself.

The learning. Control is a natural human tendency, but ineffective as a leadership strategy. Influence is a powerful resource in navigating change. Exercising personal dominion over the way I show up is within my ability to control. As a I serve in a role, but I don't *own* the job - I own the work I do and how I perform, but the job is simply a vehicle through which I serve for a period of time (in an interim or permanent role).

Determine how I can Make a Difference as a Leader Right Now

It's exciting to begin a new role with a fresh start, new goals, and aspirations personally and for the organization. I've learned it is easy to over commit to aggressive goals to advance a business quickly. My anecdote: deconstruct how to make the most of each day.

Adjusted for holidays and weekends, there are about 248 business days each year, 62 days per quarter, roughly 21 operating days per month. Most executives estimate 70%-80% of their time is not allocated at their discretion (meaning they are subject to mandatory meetings, administrative tasks, time required by other stakeholders, audits, and the like). That distills into 13 days per quarter (in aggregate) to make an impact on the business; roughly 110 - 130 hours. **The strategic leadership question I ask myself is: How will I invest those hours to make my most meaningful impact?**

How will I influence selection of the most impactful activities, performed effectively, each available hour this month to move the business as far as possible in the direction toward our long-term vision? Here are three ideas that help me address this question:

- **De-emphasize the annual calendar.** It may seem counterintuitive yet managing exclusively to the annual plan has drawbacks. Big goals can be overwhelming. Deconstructing each into digestible pieces that play to a team's competencies makes goals more manageable and better informs the activities necessary for successful fulfilment.

  While a company's vision changes infrequently, the path to its fulfilment can change as conditions shift. Managing to monthly goals enables greater flexibility when early signs of changing conditions emerge. The best strategic plan is one that guides daily discretionary activities executed in alignment with the long-term vision.

- **Compare plans with activity capacity.** Deconstructing annual and strategic plans into daily activities, performed in increments of 21 business days, enables leaders to ask: How does the plan compare with our capacity to perform required activities? Can we realistically perform this set of tasks effectively over the next calendar month?

Understanding capacity is a powerful foundation for establishing goals, even those requiring a stretch. *Good to Great* author Jim Collins describes "Big Hairy Audacious Goals" as a powerful mechanism to stimulate progress, as they require building for the long term and exuding a relentless sense of urgency *today*. Leaders must combine the drive to achieve aspirational goals with a clear understanding of the organization's capacity. From there, we must allocate capacity for the highest, greatest application of all resources.

- **Daily gut checks.** Perhaps the greatest challenge leaders face is managing their attention. Continuous distractions operate like an undercurrent pulling us from our focus. Much of our time is not within our control. Leader effectiveness is heavily impacted by use of discretionary time — that portion of your calendar you do control. Apply attention during discretionary time to those activities where you can have the greatest impact and contribute the largest ROI. Gut check questions are:
  - Where will I add the greatest value to the organization today?
  - How do I make the most of my discretionary time today in alignment with the organization's goals?
  - Which activities will have the lowest ROI from investing my attention, and should be avoided?

Leaders set the tone through focus and alignment with organizational priorities. Making our time count enhances productivity and demonstrates strategic leadership daily.

The learning: Making a difference as a leader right now means aligning today's activities with the organization's vision. Everything else follows vision: priorities, activities, processes, and results. From there, I can intentionally invest my discretionary time in the activities which will have the greatest impact on advancing the business.

The core theme throughout this book is this: with perpetual motion in business as the norm, leaders hold responsibility for navigating continually changing conditions. Navigating change is simply business as usual; it's not a special event. A deep understanding of this principle provides leaders with a strategic management paradigm. My hope is this book has helped elevate your acumen in *Leading from Now!*

www.ingramcontent.com/pod-product-compliance
Lightning Source LLC
Chambersburg PA
CBHW060617200326
41521CB00007B/794